UNDERSTANDING
ECONOMICS

UNDERSTANDING ECONOMICS

HARLAN M. SMITH

M.E.Sharpe

Armonk, New York
London, England

Library of Congress Cataloging-in-Publication Data

Smith, Harlan M., 1914–
Understanding economics / Harlan M. Smith.
p. cm.
Includes bibliographical references and index.
ISBN 0-7656-0483-3 (hc. : alk. paper) ISBN 0-7656-0484-1 (pbk : alk. paper)
1. Economics. I. Title.
HB171.S664 1999
330—dc21 99-21207
CIP

Printed in the United States of America

The paper used in this publication meets the minimum requirements of
American National Standard for Information Sciences—
Permanence of Paper for Printed Library Materials,
ANSI Z 39.48-1984.

BM (c) 10 9 8 7 6 5 4 3 2 1

Table of Contents

Preface

Although economics could not be more important than it is in everyone's life, not many people really understand the subject. Some were scared off from studying it for one reason or another, and others never even had a good opportunity. Some learned economics from standard textbooks alone, and are somewhat the worse off as a result—they did not learn it properly. Some of what they learned was based on economists' oversimplified models of the economy. They need to start all over. If they learn it properly, they will understand both economics and the economy better.

Some people think they know enough economics as a result of their job experience, or from their experience as a consumer, but they could be the worst off of all. What is learned from personal experience is often very valuable in adding to knowledge about how the economy affects some people, but it is dangerous to generalize about the whole complex economy on the basis of any one person's limited experience.

The fact is that everyone is better off by really understanding economics, which is the reason for this little book. It isn't possible to know everything about the economy from one single book, let alone a short book like this one. But the author contends that this book will help you understand more than the standard textbook alone will.

This little book was written for three types of readers: (1) those who wish to understand economics well without taking a college course, (2) those currently taking an introductory principles of economics course, and (3) those who took an economics course some time ago and are ready to rethink what they can properly take from it and remember.

This book can readily help all three types of readers. Its organization roughly parallels that of standard principles of economics textbooks, but it will help you understand important things about economics better.

The book starts with the usual argument that everyone needs to know some economics, and distinguishes misuses of economics from good economics. This is followed by showing how some introductory economics concepts need to be treated if they are to be learned properly.

The central concept of the subject is that of economizing, assuming rationality on the part of people as both producers and consumers. Four chapters in this book discuss both the value and the limitations of the standard textbook analysis.

Then a whole section deals with what we really need to learn about demand and supply, about competition, and about Adam Smith's concept of the invisible hand that makes private good and public good coincide through competition.

Textbooks usually explain the elementary mysteries of money and finance, but fail to explain their influence upon the economy or stress the problem of regulating their safety as this book does.

All textbooks treat monopoly as well as competition, but they often do not give you, as this book will, a real understanding of the degree of uncertainty in business management or of the current influence of Wall Street, in disregard of various stakeholders, on how business operates.

Textbook treatment of income and wealth distribution badly needs to be rethought—again, this little book will help you understand it properly.

The economics profession's controversies in the field of macroeconomics are dealt with here so you can learn to understand macroeconomics too.

This book concludes with sections on the global economy, the future development of economies and economic systems, and the future of economics as a discipline.

To use this book with or without a standard textbook will certainly help your thinking about economics and your understanding of it. You will learn how to evaluate the simple assumptions underlying economists' models. You will be presented with a more realistic view of the economy, how it works, and the issues that people need to consider— issues that economists often sweep under the rug by the assumptions they make in their analyses. Read this book, and enjoy learning economics properly presented.

If you do use this book with a textbook that discusses topics in a somewhat different order from that assumed here, you will have no difficulty in altering the order in which you read some chapters in this book. It will usually be best to read your standard textbook chapter first, and then read the appropriate chapter here. This book will induce you to consider issues in a broader framework and help you avoid some common oversimplifications of economic issues. If your instructor bases multiple choice tests on the standard textbook, your grade depends upon answering in terms of that textbook. Your education will profit, however, by knowing what is in this book as well.

UNDERSTANDING ECONOMICS

1. Why Study Economics?

People study economics, as they study any subject, for two major reasons: (1) to increase their understanding of some aspect of the world around them—that is, understanding for its own sake—and (2) to be able to act more wisely in their own personal economic behavior, and, in their citizenship roles, to make more intelligent decisions with respect to public policies. Understanding the economy involves getting a realistic picture of it and being able to discriminate among explanations (theories) as to why it behaves as it does. Such understanding is necessary if one is to intelligently apply certain principles in action, whether pursuing certain objectives (values) in one's occupational role, or in one's role as a consumer, a member of some group or organization, or a citizen.

So the questions are: Does economics *describe* the economy and the economic aspect of life realistically? Are these *explained* adequately and properly? How can economics be generally *useful* and helpful in the several roles in which it is needed? How to *prevent* it from sometimes being misleading and harmful or even dangerous by virtue of the conclusions that are sometimes drawn from it or for some purposes?

Those are questions which will be dealt with here, initially by examining the definition, character, and misuses of economics in general, and then by examining certain specific economic ideas in much more detail. The hope is that this will induce a more careful assessment of some economics and more care in applying results of abstract analysis to a complicated world, without losing the real value of the discipline. That value lies partly in the training it gives in systematic thinking and

3

in logical reasoning. We must remember, as we explore the generalizations of economists and their critics, that all generalizations are at best only part truths, and the question is always whether the more important part has been included or excluded. John Maurice Clark, in his old age considered by some to be a sort of dean of economists, once claimed that if we assumed the opposite of the common economists' assumptions when they developed their theories, we would also have part of the truth.[1] For example, economists assume rational behavior. If instead we assumed people are emotional and irrational, that would also be partly true, for human nature is quite complex. A very different analysis would follow from a different assumption. Assuming complex human nature would not permit the simple theories that economists have developed.

Every social problem has an economic dimension, but there are also noneconomic considerations in every policy choice. Both need attention. Can efficiency and equity be reconciled? How can the common interest prevail over the special interest? How can social costs be minimized? Indeed, what are the opportunity costs, the trade-offs in every relevant dimension, of doing something? Can employment or productivity be increased in doing it? The analytical approach of economics should consider such things, as well as comparing short and long runs. It needs to embody both marginal analysis and globalism. Consider how well economics is doing the job and what could be done better.

2. The Definition, Character, and Misuse of Economics

Read this near the beginning of an economics course to be forewarned of some dangers, and read it again as you finish an economics course when you can put more substance on the bones of the argument.

One might expect the definition of the discipline to be a simple matter on which agreement would be widespread. Indeed there seems to be a fairly common conception implicit in the work of economists, but it turns out to be difficult to formulate that in simple terms, so textbooks differ somewhat in their definitions of economics. How the field is defined can make a difference in the character of the subject. Edwin R.A. Seligman sheds some light on the argument about definition: "Economics, which has long been and will perhaps ever continue to be the battle ground of rationalizations for group and class interests, has suffered more than any other discipline from the malaise of polemics about definition and method."[2]

One might suppose that a definition of economics should include analyses of all types of economic systems, preindustrial economies as well as different modern economies. It is not easy to formulate such a definition. Many of the textbook definitions are somewhat restrictive. For example, if the field is defined as the study of how buying and selling activities organize people's efforts to make a living, the subject is almost confined to a study of so-called market economies and indeed to only parts of them.

An old definition was that economics is the study of the social organization of human want-satisfying activity. This should get around the shortcomings of definitions that do not embrace all non-market aspects of economies. It should have the merit of showing alternative ways that human want-satisfying activities are pursued, along with the operation of markets. It could thus open up questions about why one method or another is used to pursue different wants in one culture or another. It could also avoid the artificial academic line drawn between some activities customarily labeled economic and others labeled noneconomic even though they are also ways of pursuing human satisfactions, ways to which the economic principle is sometimes applicable. However, economics is not ordinarily studied with this broad a scope. It usually abstracts from much social organization of human want-satisfying activity some portion of it customarily but somewhat arbitrarily called the economic system.

Then there are the definitions that focus, significantly, upon the decision-making process in using scarce resources to accomplish given objectives. Usually, however, this does not lead to empirical study of actual decision-making by households, firms, or other organizations, including government, in decisions that affect the economy. Instead of a descriptive discipline, this definition usually leads to a prescriptive analysis. It shows how to economize in the use of scarce resources; it applies a principle that shows how to maximize the attainment of a given objective. The principle involved can be applied by an individual in personal economic decisions, or by management in a business. This can have great value. But in the discipline of economics, it tends to exclude from consideration the study of how the concrete objectives are formulated in the first place and how the economic process modifies them. Instead it takes objectives and ends as given.

The definition does, however, result in a proper emphasis on economizing and on limited applications of the principle of marginalism. Actually the principle can be treated as very widely applicable. Anything can be treated as an economic problem if the objective is known and the resources to pursue it are limited. We can economize in use of our time or our energy, as well as the use of other scarce resources. There is merit in showing the widespread applicability of the principle.

However, some problems may arise in this connection and may not be treated adequately in a textbook. Economists sometimes treat many social problems as resolvable into simple applications of the principle, ignoring the problems' real social complexities. Every social problem requires going far beyond simple economic principles in order to know how best to handle it. When all else relevant is known, the economics needs to be considered along with everything else. There is also a further problem. Economists sometimes do not emphasize that there is no very simple application of the principle for economic decisions under uncertainty, which is indeed the general case. No one knows the future, but decisions are made with respect to a future that is not only not known but is inherently and necessarily uncertain. Yet that is the way we have to operate, under uncertainty.

More importantly, once the economic principle has been seen in its broad applicability even to time and energy, all human life may appear to be just one big economic problem. Students need to understand why it is easy but dangerously misleading to look at it that way. The economic principle, marginalism, does apply whenever we are certain of the end we seek, and know the limited resources available to achieve it. But how are the ends to be chosen throughout life? They are not among the "givens." They are not predetermined somehow and just arrive in our heads. We do, in fact, choose the ends we seek from time to time, as well as choose the means toward those ends. Advertisers spend a lot of money trying to influence our choices of means, but in the process are often trying also to influence the ends we seek.

Life's resources are limited, but the ends for which they are used are not predetermined. Life is not just a matter of trying to maximize satisfaction from a given set of resources. There may be many different ways to maximize our satisfaction. We need to seek the best source of our satisfaction at different stages of life. Indeed we need to ask ourselves if maximizing our personal satisfaction is the end we should always seek above all else. Is not life best regarded as seeking wisdom as to how to live at each stage in life? What is wise at any stage of life to do with our time and energy and monetary resources? Is the quality of life really reducible to one-dimensional utility maximization? After a little serious reflection, would we not agree that the economic principle is widely but not universally applicable—it does not swallow up all life?

This raises the question of what it is that economics should do. What purposes should it serve? To what should it contribute? What have been the purposes economists thought they served? What are the discipline's implicit values?

A definition of much economics would exclude all reference to how people actually make decisions and all implications that the behavior of any actual economy was being studied, for much economics is simply a study of the logical implications of certain abstractly conceived economic models, models born in the minds of economists. They exhibit varying degrees of unreality. Models, which are primarily sets of assumed relationships among selected economic variables, may be fascinating intellectual toys but should not be employed as if they have direct and unqualified practical applicability. It can be very misleading and result in inappropriate policies if the model is taken to be a picture of reality. Indeed models can be constructed to give almost any conclusion desired, and then be used to argue for certain policies in actual economies as though economics had proven what the results of choosing or rejecting the policy would be. What the model can prove is the results that would be in the model, but not in the economy that the model may or may not sufficiently resemble. In any case, a model should not be treated as a norm, consciously or unconsciously. Taking something to be a norm should require explicit consideration of various value criteria.

The value of an economic model is to teach rigorous thinking about the logical implications of assumptions about economic relationships. The temptation of the model builder is to make assumptions that make the model simpler and hence to make the problems to which it may be applied readily solvable. Such solutions are highly suspect. But if an economic model leaves out only less important relationships, and has a close approximation to the real relationships among some important variables, it may give some valuable insights, though partial and limited, into certain factors in an economy. The simpler the model, however, the more important things it leaves out in this very complicated and interrelated world. Mathematical formulation of a model permits the mind to grasp a larger set of relationships than otherwise, promotes rigorous analysis, and may conduce to empirical testing of hypotheses. However, not everything relevant can always be properly expressed in mathematical formulas, and danger lies in overreliance on the apparent finality of mathematically deduced conclusions.

The model can be especially misleading if there is insufficient attention to the results' sensitivity to changes in the parameters, or to the effect of introducing additional relationships. A fairly simple model of business fluctuations, for example, exhibits equilibrium tendencies, or damped cycles, or explosive cycles, depending upon small changes in its parameters. That makes it necessary to know a lot about their actual magnitudes and the causes of any changes in those magnitudes. There is no substitute for knowing a lot about the economy in order to use a model safely.

Models can be helpful when they give some correct though limited insights into the operation of an economy, but it is dangerous to misuse them. A model is misused when conclusions are drawn from it and then acted upon as though they were drawn from and applicable without qualification to the actual complicated economy. It is a misuse to develop them to argue for preconceived policies or as a substitute for direct study of actual decision-making and the behavior of actual economies.

Governmental economic policies can have such an impact on people that it is not simply an economist's self-serving bias to contend that everyone needs to have a reasonably good understanding of the economy today. Economic education has accordingly been extended in many school systems from higher education down to the elementary level. What is taught is, for the most part, fairly standard and widely accepted economics. This could be valuable. Yet there is reason to question whether some of the standard analysis is not sometimes doing more harm than good in being widely disseminated if it is in the form of much simplified models that are said to prove the correctness of major policy conclusions.

This places much responsibility upon the economics profession to carry on enough internal criticism so that these biases can be laid bare, since the public is in general unable to uncover the hidden assumptions that bias the results. Even college students majoring in economics do not generally question seriously the economics being taught. Thus they are in danger of mistaking some of its conclusions, so rigorously arrived at, as dicta about the real world to be applied in simple and direct fashion to situations very much more complicated than the models, and involving many human issues that the models did not embody (perhaps because the economists did not consider them). Since the world is very complicated and cannot be grasped in its entirety, we inevitably abstract in picturing the world. The problem arises when we omit something of vital importance in order to simplify a model, instead of omitting only things of minor relevance.

There are times when anyone trying to understand the economy and any student of the discipline of economics needs to be as realistic as possible. We need to recognize that economics does not typically consider all the ways that people (individually and in businesses, organizations, and governments) behave or act to pursue their desires, let alone the sources and alterations of their desires. The cultures and the institutions in which these behaviors and desires operate are left to other disciplines to study, although they affect in very important ways what we abstractly call the economy. The historical ranges, changes, and present ranges of combinations of what might be called economic matters exceed what the discipline considers for the most part.

The study of economic ideas is important because they influence our behaviors, so some attention should be paid to the ideologies (ideas, value systems, and emotions) that are part of the different cultural patterns from which economics often abstracts rather sharply.

What used to be called institutional economics at least had the merit of considering the actual institutional framework and its relation to the economic forces operating in actual economies. This could lead to better understanding of the real world and less danger of mistaking an abstract model for the real world, with consequently less danger of adopting policies that ignored complications excluded from the model.

Another danger stemming from the preoccupation of modern economics with abstract models is something another approach to economics is trying to correct, as indicated by the phrase "economics as if people mattered." The charge against standard modern economics is that economists get so wrapped up in and committed to market concepts and market-measured efficiency concepts that they forget that what really matters is what happens to people who are affected by the forces being discussed so mechanically.

Economics as sometimes defined now is called a positive science rather than a normative one. That is, it purports to describe what is, not what somebody thinks ought to be. It is defined as a science of the relation of means to ends and as excluding from consideration the choice of ends. That does not mean that it is useful only for understanding and that it is irrelevant for policy purposes. Its usefulness for the latter purposes is found in its clarification of the relation of means to ends.

It is argued that one may not be able to choose ends wisely without an understanding of the means entailed in seeking various ends. All this is defensible, but in fact much of what economists are involved in nowadays is better termed political economy, as of old, for they are often pronouncing judgments upon policies in terms that are not devoid of normative elements. Of course, as human beings, economists are appropriately and necessarily making value judgments, but they seldom make clear that their conclusions are tied to their value judgments rather than being dictated solely by a positive (and supposedly value-free) analysis.

Of course, students do not want to learn economics based simply on the values of a particular economist, values that perhaps would not be widely shared. They deserve to be taught objective economic analysis in the sense that it would be agreed to by economists with different economic philosophies. Presumably dropping the earlier term "political economy" in favor of the term "economics" implied a desired but artificial narrowing of the subject to positive economics. Positive economics, insofar as it is possible to be objective and independent of economic philosophy, can have a useful role, as has just been argued. However, the pretense of complete objectivity in economics needs to be abandoned. While it is desirable to know economics independently of some particular economic philosophy, it should be clear that value premises are implicit throughout the discipline. They should generally be made explicit. The very choice of problems to be addressed involves a value judgment. And every choice of programs or policies involves some value judgments in close conjunction with the economic analysis.

The student and the citizen receiving an economist's advice on policy issues has every right to know the economic philosophy of that economist. If they share that economic philosophy in at least the relevant aspects, they can find the advice useful. If the economist's weighting of different values at the current margin is substantially different, they can appropriately disregard the advice, for it is not directed at their present set of relative values and objectives but at a somewhat different one.

There is every reason society should expect economists to help contribute to bettering the economic system. A better economics might be able to contribute to that objective too, if economists would accept some responsibility in that respect. In fact, much attention continues to be focused on economic policy issues even from economists prominent in advocating positive economics. Although some economics and some economists ignore or fail to be helpful in dealing with our social problems, economics should be able to shed some light on the problems. But it can readily be misused in just this connection. In some books economists give their prescriptions for more than a dozen social problems in a matter of a few pages for each, drawing conclusions from economic models and without making clear their values and their economic philosophy, and without careful consideration of the real complexities of the problems. When complicated social problems are treated as one-dimensional economic problems, economics is being misused to give lopsided answers that may be given too much weight. Perhaps economics is not the right discipline for pronouncing on our social problems at all, but then what discipline is? As it is, other disciplines also take a crack at the social problems, each from its own limited vantage point. How nice it would be if the problems were such that they could be broken down into separate and unrelated aspects, each of which could be studied separately by an appropriate discipline, and the results of the separate studies then simply added together to give a comprehensive view of a problem and an adequate resolution of it. But the world's problems are not like that. What may be needed is a group of scholars specializing in a limited number of social problems in their manifold complexity. Meanwhile it behooves economists and other social scientists to be more careful about how simply and directly applicable are any of their recommendations to complex social problems.

Economics is now being misused in another way. Instead of economists' trying to learn something from the other social sciences and thereby attempting to improve their own analyses, we see a form of economic imperialism, with attempts being made to reduce to economic terms the behaviors ordinarily treated in the other social sciences.

Economics has been accused, not without reason, of constituting a vast rationalization of the socioeconomic status quo, now and throughout the earlier history of the discipline. Or more specifically as a rationalization of business's freedom to do whatever it likes, on the ground that this will be in the general interest, or on the ideological ground that there is an inherent right involved that can't be interfered with. Yet economists often have the reputation in the business community of being antibusiness radicals. The paradox is at least partly explained by the interest of many economists in mild reforms to improve the performance of the economy with respect to those near the bottom end of the economic ladder. Many in the profession have had such a concern, while stoutly defending the economic system as such. Many others earn their living directly as business economists.

Not all the latest in economics is to be taken as great progress, however. As business schools go from one set of buzzwords to another, academic economists also are subject to fads or fashions and swings in outlook and terminology. These may be harmless if not taken too seriously. There is, of course, never harm in being able to see things from different perspectives, too limited and somewhat distorting though some may be, for there may often be some sparks of light that can be seen only thus. Acquaintance with different economic views may add something to the understanding of reality and the complex mixture of things that it is. And it is necessary to recognize how differently that reality is seen by different people, and yet to be able to analyze each viewpoint critically.

A Simplified Model

In the following pages attention will be paid to considerations that may be missed in drawing conclusions from a simple economic model. An example of a basic economic model may be summarized as follows:

The underlying determinants of an economy's behavior are the people's economic motivation, their wants, the resources available to serve those wants, the technology that connects the two, and the money supply. Together they explain the whole economy. They underlie the demand and supply (curves) of outputs and productive inputs, and which demands and supplies determine (relative) prices of outputs and inputs (the latter prices including wage rates), while the money supply determines the price level. Such an economy efficiently maximizes consumer want satisfaction as firms competitively seek to maximize their profits.

Of course, textbooks elaborate the concepts employed and the relationships and behavior assumed. We will not deal with these in the same way. Most of our comments will be intended to induce thinking about some aspects of the economics and of the conclusions thus developed from economic models.

Some Introductory Concepts

3. How Some Basic Things Are Determined by an Economic System

It is customary to list three basic things that every economic system determines: (1) what to produce, (2) how to produce it, and (3) for whom to produce it. The analysis then indicates how each of these determinations is made in a given type of economic system, and may indicate alternative ways. The first two may be combined as the allocation of productive resources and the third designated as the distribution of income. These are indeed basic. Three other basic determinations are made, although one might try to sneak them in under the initial three categories. An economic system determines the level of employment of labor, varying as that level may be from time to time in some economies. This is of such importance that it should be added as a fourth thing determined by any economic system. Although economists find the equilibrium concept analytically very useful, disequilibria at both micro and macro levels is in a sense more normal, which raises question five as to how any economic system deals with situations when things are "out of kilter"; attention needs to be focused on the determination of the outcomes of various disequilibria. A sixth thing determined by any economic system may be implicitly assumed under resource allocation, but is of such importance that it might better be listed separately to be sure it gets explicit attention; that is, the determination of the provisions made for the future. This embraces the rate of saving and investment, technological research and development, and, as we have become more aware recently, the sustainability of a local or national or even world economy. Sustainability is affected by pollution, overloading the life-support system, and depletion of natural resource capital.

A common textbook treatment classifies economic systems as traditional, command, and market systems. In the first type of system, the above basic things are determined by tradition; there are customary ways of doing everything. Simple preindustrial economies are characterized thus. By contrast, command economies are illustrated by centrally planned communist economies where the basic determinations are made by government officials and carried out by government command. The third alternative is for the basic determinations to be made by markets, that is, through buying and selling activities. Indeed one may get the idea that all economic activity is being carried on according to custom in the traditional economic system, and by command in the command type of economy, and by buying and selling in market type economies.

Such a picture is misleading, for although there are large and contrasting differences among the three types of economies characterized by the dominant roles of three factors—custom, command, and market —all three factors play a significant role in every economy. The task of the student of economics is to identify the roles of each even where they are sometimes unnoticed, at least by textbook treatments. These comments will be confined to a few illustrations in command and market economies.

Consider first the role of custom in a market economy. We sometimes speak of setting the price for a product as involving the customary markup over cost. When collective bargaining in some industries results in a certain percentage wage increase, this has quite an influence on the outcome in many other industries, in order to maintain the customary pattern of relative wages. Much of the economy is not a matter of market prices, but of household production, and recreational and organizational activities. These follow cultural patterns that are traditional in the culture. Once one begins to think about this sort of thing, some other illustrations will probably come to mind to show that custom does indeed play a role in our market economy.

Market plays a role in the major command economies. Not every product is rationed; there are retail stores in which things are sold and bought in a consumer goods market. Indeed not all labor is conscript labor: People are hired and paid wages; that is a sort of labor market, despite its being more restricted than our labor markets.

Command plays an important role in our market economy, though that role has been somewhat modified over the years. There was a day when an employer hired an employee, but once hired the employee could be and was ordered to do as he was told, and failing compliance would simply be fired. Command is still alive and well in business hierarchies, but it was much qualified by the rise of effective unions to check arbitrary use of management power, and sometimes more recently by management openness to input from employees. And, of course, government always has some commands, often of the "thou shalt not" variety.

Custom can give a degree of stability in some respects, though it can be a drag upon needed change at times; evaluation of its role needs to be on a case-by-case basis. It is human nature to object to being commanded, so minimization of the role of command is readily recommended, but there are circumstances where command is not only more efficient but is finally necessary. There have to be order-givers and order-takers after even democratic decisions have been made. Markets have the advantage of economizing on consensus and of permitting proportional representation in determining what shall be produced, and so on. But in addition to what the textbooks call market failure, it is obvious that there are some important things that we don't want to have decided through markets—for example, we don't buy and sell spouses or children, and the slave market is now anathema.

Custom, command, and market are mechanisms used in all economies in different ways and in different proportions. Their relative merits in different specific roles is worth considering.

4. *Caeteris Paribus* and Prediction

One of the most important concepts in economics is the concept of *caeteris paribus,* the Latin term used to mean roughly "other things remaining the same." The term is indeed important in any science, for virtually any theorem stating causal relations among a limited number of variables needs to include the term *caeteris paribus.* Although the term is often not explicitly stated with the theorem, it needs to be attached to it at least implicitly. But the concept is a source of confusion for many students. The reason for discussing it here is to make explicit a real issue, as well as to try to clarify for the student both its significance and the difficulty of proving or disproving economists' theories, matters to which some books devote insufficient attention. Comments will be made about the nature and the significance of predictions as tests of theories.

It is necessary in stating a theory on the causal relation between two variables to abstract from other economic changes, "locking them" in caeteris paribus. The problem is that sometimes too much may be hidden in caeteris paribus, including some things that cannot legitimately be treated as unaffected and hence remaining the same. A case in point will be discussed below (see essay 28) in connection with the debate between Keynesian and classical theories of unemployment.

Let us take here as an illustration of the issues involved a simple statement of a quantity theory of money. The theory as stated here is that any change in the money supply changes the price level in the same direction and in the same proportion. We leave aside, as though settled, what money supply measure is intended and what price level is allegedly thus affected. If taken as a simple predictive proposition, we can readily ascertain that it is frequently wrong. Indeed it is not meant as a simple predictive proposition, but as a statement of a causal relationship. The purport is to say that a causal relation of the sort indicated does indeed exist. (It would be a more far-reaching proposition to say that all price-level changes can be explained solely by changes in the money supply, implying as that would that nothing else can affect the price level.) But here we stay with the simple causal statement relating changes in M to resulting proportional changes in P in the same direction.

The caeteris paribus term is at least an implicit part of the theory, but can well be made explicit. Caeteris paribus (i.e., other things remaining the same), changes in M cause the indicated changes in P. The theory takes into account the fact that any unit of money turns over repeatedly as it is used for numerous successive transactions. The turnover of money in a period is called its velocity (VH), and the number of transactions in a period is abbreviated as T. This is summarized in the equation of exchange: $MV=PT$. It now appears that if V and T remain the same, the quantity theory is not a causal proposition at all but is reduced to a truism because the total value of money transactions in a period is equal to the total value of money transactions in a period, that total being obtained either by multiplying the amount of money used by the number of times each dollar is used on the average, or by multiplying the number of money transactions by their average price.

However, the explicit addition of caeteris paribus to the quantity theory previously stated is not to reduce the theory to a truism but to isolate the causal relation asserted from other influences that may throw off a simple prediction. If indeed the quantity theory, or any theory in any discipline, were valid only in a world in which nothing else changed, it would be worthless. That is not the consequence of stating each theory caeteris paribus. The purpose is to abstract from other changes going on in the world, changes about which that theory is making no statements.

That brings us to the difficulty of testing a theory empirically. It is obviously not sufficient to support a causal theory to find an instance or a few instances in which the relation appears to hold, though that is a common way unsophisticated advocates of any theory try to prove its validity for the public, and the public is sometimes gullible enough to be convinced by such proofs. What appears more convincing is an indication that the theory seems to hold generally. Even such a finding does not warrant stating it as universally true, because no limited number of instances can prove that a proposition is a universally true proposition. It cannot be proven by empirical data from past and present that the future might not turn up exceptions. Something generally true to date would, however, be significant unless some foreseeable changes would be expected to alter the relationship. The usual way to see how often an asserted relationship holds, such as the quantity theory of money being discussed, is to gather data on the changes in the money supply and in the price level (measured in some appropriate way) and to see how closely the two sets of changes are related to one another over a substantial period of time. The usual measure is a coefficient of correlation. A perfect correlation would have the numerical value of one, and a complete absence of correspondence in movements of the two variables would show a coefficient of zero. Coefficients close to one would seem on the face of the matter to validate the quantity theory. However, even this is no proof of the theory, although this sort of evidence is popularly taken to be adequate proof of any theory. But correlation gives no indication of causation. The causal relation could run from changes in P to changes in M, rather than as the quantity theory posited, or the high correlation might result from both M and P being made to change together because both are a result of some third factor not even in the equation. For example, bankers have sometimes claimed that it is not their increasing the money supply that causes prices to rise, but rather that when other factors cause prices to rise, people find it necessary to borrow more from the banks in order to carry on business at the higher price level, and so the money supply expands because prices rose. This would be as consistent with a high correlation between M and P as the quantity theory would be.

While a single instance where a supposedly universal proposition does not hold is sufficient to invalidate it as a universal, a single instance where a posited relation does not hold does not necessarily invalidate a theory as a generalization or generally true proposition. Again we have an example of the sort of disproof of propositions that is often offered to and probably accepted by the public. Some newspaper account might tell of an instance where the price level did not change in proportion to the change in the quantity of money, and this would be cited as proof that the quantity theory was no good.

But another matter is involved here besides the difference between a universal proposition and one generally true. If the quantity theory were really a predictive proposition, then of course the theory failed in this instance: The predicted did not happen. But a causal proposition is not the same as a prediction. Caeteris paribus is part of a causal proposition. The quantity-theory proposition says that the effect of a change in the quantity of money is to change the price level by the same proportion (and in the same direction). Other things may also operate on the price level at the same time, which will be reflected in changes in V or T in the equation of exchange, and that may explain why the P did not change in the same proportion as the M. If such is the case, the quantity theory may still be valid. The amount of change in P that was due to change in M can be augmented by or offset to some degree by other factors that change independently of the change in the quantity of money. What caeteris paribus adds is that the causal relation asserted abstracts from those other independent changes and enables one to assert merely the effect of the change in one variable M. All this, of course, makes it much more difficult to disprove a statement about a causal relationship by finding an instance or even numerous instances where it does not appear to hold.

What would be required to disprove the quantity theory as stated would be a finding that changes in the quantity of money had either direct or indirect influences on the velocity of circulation of money (V) or upon the volume of transactions (T) or, more accurately, on the V/T ratio. We think there is some such evidence, at least, for short-run changes in M. The intent here, however, is not a full discussion of the quantity theory of money and of how well or how poorly one formulation or another of such theories fits the rest of the body of economic analysis that is our presently held approximation to a satisfactory explanation of economic phenomena. The theory is used here merely to discuss the significance of the caeteris paribus assumption in economics at a little greater length than is usual in the textbooks, both because of its general importance and because the usual explanation often leaves students with an insufficiently clear understanding of what its significance is. More than incidentally, it may be added here that much of what economists accept (or scientists in other disciplines accept) is a matter of how well a given theorem fits with the rest of what is currently generally accepted in the discipline. For often that is the best evidence we have of its likely validity.

The above comments may also serve to shed some light upon the concept that economics is a discipline in which the test of a theory is its ability to predict. It is argued by some economists that the unreality of assumptions in a theory is irrelevant if it predicts well. However, the test of how well it predicts is a matter of how well it would have predicted at certain times in the past. That is to say, the theory is formulated so that it fits data on the past, hence is one possible explanation of the past. There may be alternative theories that would equally well explain some of the past, that is, predict some part of it from a previous part of it. Some in the profession contend that the chances that one theory or another will have predictive value for the unknown future depend first upon the degree of realism of the assumptions on which the theory rests, and second upon how significant are the unpredictable changes that may occur in relationships that have held in the past.

Much of the trouble we have been discussing arises, of course, out of the fortunate inability of the economist (and social scientists generally) to conduct the sort of scientifically controlled experiments that are sometimes possible in the natural sciences. People are fortunate that they do not have to serve as guinea pigs for social science experiments designed to prove or disprove some hypotheses.

Yet the fact remains that we need as much light as we can get on various theories about causal relationships among economic variables in order to know the most likely consequences of various economic policies which, from time to time, may be chosen in various circumstances. Choices have to be made on the basis of judgments about various theories, despite lack of definitive proof about their validity in the past and certainly without proof about how well they may hold in the future. So theories are indispensable for action as well as for providing some understanding of events. A purely descriptive economics would only lead to questions as to what explains why things are as they are or were as they were. One can fill books with statistical data or other descriptive data, and they would be utterly boring to read unless accompanied by some effort at explanation, and anything offered as an explanation of anything is a theory. So we cannot escape the problems of the validity of theories, however troublesome and undefinitive the results.

What we can do and need to do is try to formulate theories that start with as full as possible a recognition of the actual facts that need to be explained, rather than ignoring the degree of unreality of the theories that we spin to give us a simple model we might prefer to reason about. The actual behavior of markets, of business decision-makers, of household consumers, of workers, and others needs to be examined first-hand, along with the perceptions of decision-makers and their possibly complex set of motives. A lot of contemporary economics is study of the logical implications of models that are based on simplifying assumptions. Starting instead from extensive research into real behavior and relationships that there is some reason to expect will continue to hold at least in the near future should give a better basis for predictions, though at best our ability to predict the future is not going to be very great in the field of economics. There are too many ways that people can do the unexpected. Indeed economic prediction cannot be made independent of the reactions to predictions. Some predictions, despite insufficient basis, can become self-fulfilling prophecies because of people's reactions to the predictions. In other instances, even well-based predictions can lead to actions that prevent their becoming true, because people did not like what they foresaw and acted to make the future different. We do need, however, to try to ascertain the most likely effects of different actions. For this purpose, the more realistic the model, the more useful its logical implications are likely to be.

5. The Production Possibilities Frontier

Most economics principles textbooks display a production possibilities curve early in the book, showing the maximum amount of some one (conglomerate) product (such as food) that it would be possible for the economy to produce, given its resource base and technology, along with the maximum possible production of another product, again using all available resources, and all intermediate possibilities that divide the resources between the two (conglomerate) products. As stated, the concept is somewhat fanciful, because it assumes that it would be possible to have the entire economy use all its resources and confine itself to either such product.

There are several important concepts that are or can be explained with the aid of the production possibilities frontier. They can be as well or better explained by envisaging a more realistic situation, starting from an existent allocation of resources among different lines of production, a sort of multidimensional production possibilities concept instead of a two-dimensional frontier, and with attention to the concept of using all of an economy's resources.

An economy is said to be technically efficient if its production lies somewhere on the production possibilities frontier. The frontier shows the available choices of efficient combinations of products, hence the opportunity costs and possible marginal trade-offs at any point on the frontier. Think now not of end points on a two-dimensional curve, but of producing some technically efficient real combination of outputs, represented by a set of points in n-dimensions. One can think then about various possible trade-offs; increasing any one output will be at the expense of some other output or outputs. How much of any one thing would have to be sacrificed to increase the output of something else is the opportunity cost (the significant economic cost) of that increased output in terms of the specific alternative sacrificed at that particular margin. There are thus numerous possible trade-offs at any existent margin, so expansion of one output has a range of specifiable opportunity costs.

In connection with the production possibilities curve or elsewhere, textbooks usually introduce the principle of increasing opportunity costs. The more one increases the output of one thing at the expense of others, the higher the opportunity cost of the first.

An economy is not technically efficient if it could produce more of some product without reducing production of another, a situation represented by points inside the production possibilities frontier, viewed multidimensionally or more simply. The existence of involuntarily unemployed labor would indicate that many lines of production could be expanded without decreasing production anywhere, provided the labor was mobile skillwise and geographically. Involuntarily unemployed labor, when it exists, is the most serious technical inefficiency in an economy.

Full employment of other resources, usually implied by saying that the production possibilities frontier gives the maximum output possible by using all the economy's resources, does not have the importance or even the meaning that full employment of labor has. The capacity of capital equipment is itself a rather loose concept. Ordinarily capital capacity, as usually measured, is built ahead of normal operating rates partly to facilitate steady output growth instead of growth being held at a fixed limit until a large lump of capacity can be added, which again would be underutilized for a time. In short, capacity grows by lumps instead of by small steady increments. And if existent capacity is pushed to its short-run limit, that may run into higher costs, and might involve overfull employment of labor to make it possible. The proper objective for an economy is not to do whatever is necessary with people to get maximum possible output from all capital equipment in existence at any given time. The equipment is there to facilitate full and productive employment of labor in a growing economy. As for full utilization of other resources, little sense can be made of the concept of full utilization. So-called natural resources are themselves "produced"; there is no fixed supply of them to be either fully utilized or left unused, with the implication that the former is involved in maximizing the output of the economy.

Finally, a word about allocative efficiency in relation to the production possibilities frontier. The question of where to operate on the production possibilities frontier is a matter of allocative efficiency, not just technical efficiency. Allocative efficiency is a matter of getting the most highly valued combination of outputs on the frontier. This can lead to discussions of what determines the relative valuation of different output combinations, and discussion of how well an actual resource allocation coincides with an optimal set of points on the multidimensional production possibilities frontier. Some comments on the valuation problem will be made later.

6. Wants, Resources, Technology, Productive Units

Any economy can be analyzed in terms of people's wants, the resources available to satisfy those wants, and the technology that determines how many wants can be satisfied by available resources through the operation of productive organizations of one kind or another.

That sounds quite simple, but it turns out that the three elements are not entirely independent of one another. Productive organizations now include corporations and other forms of businesses, households (which produce many human wants that do not go through a market to be bought and sold), and many other social organizations that may or may not operate in part through buying and selling. Many of these productive units not only produce goods and services in response to known wants, but they make efforts to influence people to want what they produce. And the technology available is itself a product of efforts to develop better ways of producing whatever is produced. Even an economic resource depends in part on the technology. Oil was not a productive resource at one time until a technology was developed to use it as a major source of energy.

Years ago economics textbooks started with chapters on productive resources, usually classified as land, labor, and capital. Labor was treated as all alike, a uniform resource: people. Capital referred to machinery and factories and the like. Resources included not just potentially arable land, but all the usable natural resources as well, whether on the surface or buried beneath it.

Assuming technically efficient use of resources and the technology, the economic problem was how to produce from them the greatest value. The problem was to get the best resource allocation.

What is often neglected now in trying to understand economics and the operation of any economy are the problems associated with the operation of the extractive "industries." The problems associated with the industries that are trying to get the natural resources—nickel, copper, coal, and so on—in the needed usable form and quantity are not studied separately from those businesses making products from those resources.

Indeed the single most important sector of the economy dealing with a resource is agriculture, the source of food and fiber. There is an old saying that "an army travels on its stomach" but so do we all. There is nothing so important for life as food. And in this country, ever since World War I we have talked about "the farm problem," because many farmers have faced problems that were somewhat unique to their "line of business." Even today economics textbooks usually confine their treatment of agriculture and farm problems to a chapter that points out, correctly, that if public policy supports farm prices above market-determined levels, agricultural surpluses will become a problem. Farmers' problems over the years here or elsewhere cannot be dealt with adequately in this short book, but a few comments can be made to guide readers.

Worldwide agriculture takes many forms. Many farmers barely make a living as "subsistence farmers" on their small plots with primitive technology. They grow what they eat, and they eat what they grow. With any difficulty they are forced to borrow money at usurious rates from moneylenders who often keep the farmers in debt for the rest of their lives. Many other farmers till the soil for large landowners, and may also barely subsist, while the landowner usually does much better. Semifeudal conditions still exist.

American farmers have done much better, especially with fertile land in the Midwest, and with technological improvements (in machinery, soil conservation efforts, and improved seed and fertilizer) that raised farm productivity as fast as productivity grew in much of manufacturing. But in both world wars, production expanded to meet wartime demands, which fell after the wars and lowered farm prices, to the detriment of farmers. Government support of some farm product prices (especially grains) helped large commercial farmers but did not solve problems identified as farm poverty, difficulties of the family farms, natural disasters and bad years, instability of farm prices, or the worsening of prices the farmer pays relative to the prices he receives for what he can sell. Not all proposals to deal with these other problems made sense, but few were adopted, and there is an ongoing need to see whether the problems can be dealt with better.

There is no more important sector of any economy than its agricultural sector. More attention needs to be paid to its problems.

When we consider economic resources more fully, we need to distinguish between renewable resources and non-renewable resources. Some of the latter, which are part of our economy's resource base, are being depleted today at a historically unprecedented rate. That is beginning to be discussed, and will be treated briefly in this book in essay 37. In the same essay there will be a discussion of the fact that the renewable resources are also being overused, so that even our life-support system is being overloaded. Both types of resources are also being polluted, which raises the costs of using them when they can still be used at all. And although these problems are presently being created primarily by the industrial economies of the world, if the less developed economies succeed in escaping their poverty traps and come into the industrial world, the prospect is frightening because their huge and growing populations will worsen all these problems tremendously. Yet the answer is not for them to remain poverty-stricken nor for industrial countries to again become underdeveloped. However, economics is again paying some attention to its resource base and its life-support system, yet this time not just because it is basic to all economics, but because it is in trouble.

Economizing and Rationality

7. The Economic Principle

There is only one microeconomic principle, and that may be called the principle of marginalism. A major part of microeconomic analysis is devoted merely to applications of the principle. The principle is often stated differently in different applications. If dealing with consumer expenditure decisions, the formulation may be as follows: To maximize utility, allocate expenditures so as to equalize the marginal utilities of the last dollar spent in each available line of expenditure. Or to make an efficient allocation of a productive resource, allocate the resource so that its marginal productivity in all possible uses is the same. Or to maximize profits, carry production to the point where marginal revenues and marginal costs are equal. In a more general formulation it would be: Continue any activity to the point where marginal gain and marginal cost are equal if one is trying to maximize net gain. Of course, it can be argued that the last unit of activity that equalizes the two adds nothing to net gain, so the principle should be formulated in terms of inequalities, not equalities, and continue only so long as marginal gain exceeds marginal cost; and the principle is sometimes formulated in such manner. Marginal costs are merely additions to total cost, and marginal gains are additions to total gains, from carrying something one unit farther.

Although some applications may not be obvious, and the effort may be to make it appear abstruse and difficult, as by inflicting calculus upon the uninitiated, it is reducible not simply to common sense but to simple arithmetic. The principle states merely that a total increases if one adds more to it than one subtracts from it. So do not let microeconomic maximizations throw you. Examine carefully to see whether a statement formulates the principle accurately so that it reduces to simple arithmetic, and if necessary reformulate it so that is the case, but you need not be intimidated by marginal analysis, important, fundamental, and widely applicable as it is.

But how widely applicable is the economic principle of marginalism? Decisions in terms of marginal changes do make sense, and one cannot argue with the arithmetic involved. But it can be and has been objected that it is not descriptive of how people make decisions. It is prescriptive, not descriptive. If one wants to maximize something, that being the end, and the means (resources) being limited, apply the principle, for that is the only way to succeed; it is the only rational way to maximize something. It rationally relates means to that end. The economist takes utility maximization, maximization of the satisfaction of whatever wants people have, as the ultimate objective of people. And the principle has such a prominent place in market analysis, not because people rationally maximize want satisfaction all the time, but because it is a necessary part of the explanation of market behavior. Another way of stating the matter is to say that the principle tells how to economize scarce resources, and people do economize enough that the market cannot be adequately explained without giving such economizing an important role.

In discussing definitions of economics, it was suggested that there are limits to the applicability of the economic principle; that brief discussion should be reviewed here. It concluded that all life is not reducible to an economic problem. But does this mean that rationality is limited to choices of means, and is not applicable to choices of ends and objectives in life? Are values essentially matters of taste and is wisdom irrelevant in their choice? This opens up a deeper question for philosophy, and instead of suggesting how reason might be applied to value choices, the economist is more likely to leave an impression that no philosophical position has been taken in the economic discussion, when one may have been implied by or inferred from the textbook. The next section will return to the topic of want satisfaction, maximization, and rationality in a broader context.

8. The Dehumanized Utility Function and Rationality

The consumer is said to allocate his income rationally among lines of expenditure according to the marginal principle so as to maximize his satisfaction. But individuals are often in no position to really know what would yield the best results. Economists' concept of reason implies knowledge that is not really possible, according to Herbert Simon.[3] So consumer analysis is unrealistic from the beginning. However, let us examine it in further respects.

To simplify economic analysis, certainly not to explain reality, the utility functions of individuals, as described in the textbooks, usually explicitly exclude any elements involving the utilities or disutilities of other individuals. Economists picture society as a collection of atomistic individuals who interact in markets and actually make economic decisions with neither beneficent nor sadistic impulses. One would think that at least the concept of "keeping up with the Joneses" would need to be recognized in analysis of economic behavior, and indeed it may be mentioned somewhere, but not when talking about the utility function where it is clearly relevant. The perverse preference of envy destroys the nice utility maximizing outcome of the market game. But why gum up and complicate a nice simple analysis of how atomistic individuals might behave even if that would be quite different from the way humans actually behave? We might better be realistic, even if that makes the analysis more complicated.

Without conceding that psychology has a very good picture or explanation of individual or group human behavior, surely economics is relying upon a misleading abstraction from reality in its assumptions as to human behavior in the economic realm. We don't use the term "economic man" as we used to, but it is the term that has fallen into disuse, not the assumptions. People are treated as though they rationally maximized individual want satisfaction (utility) independently of other people, and it is assumed that this is only rational self-interest, and anything other than self-interest is nonexistent as well as irrational.

It is, of course, possible to treat formally every action as dictated by pure self-interest. Even what people ordinarily call unselfishness can be treated as doing just what one wanted to do, and therefore selfish. But then we need different words to distinguish the actions that are clearly dictated without reference to others, actions even deliberately against the interest of others, and actions evidently designed to benefit others. Hopefully no economist has been brought up in a family where no one gave a damn about other members and completely ignored them in all decisions made. Since that is humanly impossible, it is safe to say that no economist had such bad luck. But then what is ordinarily

considered humane and inhumane motivation might somehow be recognized along with narrowly self-interested motives and actions in
economic analysis of the actual world, and models excluding them be
seen for what they are, models of a different and far from ideal world.
Indeed it would be realistic to say that the most important element in
anyone's utility function would not lie in the area of consumption but
in relations with other people, family and friends obviously, but also in
the so-called economic world in the quality of relations with fellow-
workers and supervisors on the job.

Indeed the economist seems to build models in which all behavior is
rational in a very narrow sense. The only partial excuse for this is that
there seems to be enough rationality that it needs to be taken into
account in order to explain actual market behavior to any significant
degree. One thing that "rational" means to the economist is that individuals act intelligently (efficiently) in their own self-interest. One
might speculate on how much better off people would be nowadays if
only we did act in our own self-interest more of the time. And it is
clear from common experience that the extensive failures to do so are
not explicable simply in terms of force and fraud. People often know
better and still do not act in their own self-interest. Irrational, yes. It is
the irrationality that the whole segment of the economy involved in
advertising, and much salesmanship, depends upon and promotes. The
economist's pure self-interest model is not realistic. People do not
really try to maximize anything that could be termed self-interest in
either a narrow or a broad sense, though they clearly would be better
off if they did. That is, if they quit doing things that are hurtful to them
they would be very much better off. But there are problems with
narrow self-interest that still need to be addressed here.

There is the question of whether the equation of self-interest in a
narrow sense with rationality does not itself have some antisocial consequences. If it does, is not the economist to blame? Has he not
equated maximizing utility and maximizing profit with rational self-interest? Perhaps he has had too much influence on our culture. Or is the
economist merely borrowing the cultural ideology, and at most reinforcing it. Is it not the case that people generally do, in this culture,
take a rather narrowly defined conception of self-interest to be the only
thing rational, and hence self-justifying? And does this not hinder
recognition of the extent to which that can produce consequences that
not only harm others but boomerang and are self-defeating? Especially

since the greatest disutilities for any of us lie in suffering that others may cause us, and our greatest satisfactions come from mutuality, not only in free contract but on the emotional level in relations with other people.

All this suffers when it is considered smart to get the maximum one can out of every opportunity, and to give as little as necessary. That sounds like rational economic behavior. But in fact such an attitude in life subverts all human relationships. If people treated each other thus, it would wreck any marriage and even any friendship. And in terms of productivity with which the economist is directly concerned, the attitude is the opposite of the work ethic and constitutes a very serious drain on productivity. Can the economist's analysis not incorporate all this instead of incorporating and thus aiding and abetting a false notion of rational self-interest that has antisocial consequences?

It would not really corrupt economic analysis if self-interest were to be more realistically defined in terms of what sociologists have called the social self. The actual self-interest that we pursue includes the well-being of at least family and friends, for anyone not inhumanly narcissistic. And when people speak of "we" in different contexts, it may refer to some group to which the person belongs and is concerned about, a group the individual is proud to be a member of, resents slurs against, and tries to promote the well-being of and the objectives of. A business man or woman may be anxious about and try to promote the interests of the business class in general, and do so on ideological grounds even at some cost, as much as for any indirect gain to their individual person. In an age of nationalism, the social self typically includes the nation as such. The self in the narrower self may even be sacrificed to the nation, although in general the further one goes from the narrow self in the more inclusive social self, from closer primary ties to ever looser secondary relations, the less concern there is for those less close and the less strongly their well-being enters the individual's utility function. On the other side of the matter, insofar as our personal dislikes go as to enjoy seeing some persons' misfortunes, those feelings are also parts of our utility functions. Society, and each of us individually, has an interest in social restraints on actions based on people's satisfaction in hurting others.

In the broad sense, self-interest is a matter of what people value and devalue. Anything that increases on a net accounting the things that a person values is in that individual's self-interest and increases its total utility, if that word is to be used in an adequate sense. Values include things that are ordinarily called ideological and personal as well as what are ordinarily called economic, and since the last of these are often not the most important, an analysis that includes explicitly only the last is quite unrealistic and misleading, as well as possibly having some antisocial consequences. Indeed community depends on a substantial sharing of values.

Consumption provides utilities, work is a matter of disutility, and rationality limits the latter to what is necessary for the former, according to classical economic doctrine. Practically speaking, there are narrow limits to the possibility in our economy of choosing our work week. But anyone knows that although disutility in work is often all too real, life without work is not a great ideal either in terms of the sort of people it produces. And practically as well as ideally, much satisfaction can often be obtained in work.

Let us come back to the economic-man concept for a moment, and assume that he and she take into account all actual net utilities as considered above and applies marginal analysis in making decisions. At best this would be prescriptive counsel, not descriptive of how people actually behave. If taken as descriptive, how could it be validated or disproven? Anything people do can be said to be in accordance with their self-interest, their maximization of utility. Thus the proposition becomes essentially tautological.

So some economists give up on utility and talk only of revealed preferences. But unless one has given up on rationality as well, and on all that follows from assuming it, one is no better off. If one gives up both utility and rationality, one has thrown out the baby with the bathwater, given up all microeconomic explanation of human behavior, given up both descriptive and prescriptive microeconomics of it. How much better it would be to try to do a decent job of both, even though that would be less simple than that to which economics has reduced it.

There are those who would tell us that we are ruled by our emotions, and that reason merely rationalizes and serves the emotions. There is ample evidence for this point of view. Clearly, advertising operates not by informing us but by playing on the emotions. So the economic system cannot claim efficient satisfaction of human wants; it endeavors to create the wants it satisfies. It treats human beings like Pavlov's dog. The essence of immorality is treating others not as ends but as means to one's own benefit. Much advertising has much to answer for, especially advertising to the immature. Fortunately, most adults have at least some degree of natural skepticism of advertising claims, so they cannot be brainwashed completely, though there is evidence that they are also affected by it to some extent. The subject of people's emotional life is a big subject, not one to be treated here. But economics needs to take it into account when it is trying to be a descriptive and explanatory as well as a prescriptive science.

Most people are motivated by moral considerations to at least some extent, and by a conception of responsibility, by a notion of the sort of good person they want to be, and are not simply amoral or immoral to a larger degree. They take satisfaction in such motivation and in action consistent with it, and in shared values. The importance of all this in the utility function is hard to overestimate, for it provides the moral basis upon which the economy depends. That it is not a strong enough basis is all too obvious, but if it were quite nonexistent, as implied by the above discussion of the "smart guy" ethic, life could be reduced to a Hobbesian world, mean, nasty, brutish, and short.

So our utility function is much different from that typically pictured in economics. It includes work, play, and consumption, it includes moral values and other values, ideological commitments and care about what happens to other people. Call it all self-interest if you insist, but pay attention to the large differences in the character of behavior hidden under that term. Now the question is raised as to whether all the different sources of utility (satisfaction) are sufficiently alike in quality that they are additive, as implied in the economist's treatment of utility maximization. Sociologist Amitai Etzioni says, "Moral acts are a source of value other than pleasure. *Indeed, many are explicitly based on denial of pleasure in the name of the principle(s) involved.*"[4] He insists that a taste for honesty is not on a par with a taste for peanut butter.

The issue should not be simply disposed of. Neither will it be pursued further here except to make a suggestion that an alternative to additivity of all utilities be considered. Insofar as there may be warrant for considering some satisfactions as somewhat noncomparable and nonadditive, perhaps we should consider the concept of better and worse balances among such qualitatively different types of satisfactions. Would this create a problem for the usual indifference curve analysis, or could it readily accommodate the balance concept?

9. Human Ends

Economics assumes that the economic man is an atomistic individual whose ends and purposes are determined outside the economic system that merely serves them. As such it avoids inquiring into human ends and so cannot really conclude, as it does, how well it serves them. For such conclusions it really needs a psychology of human needs.

Abraham Maslow's writings provide a good account of human nature. He envisages a hierarchy of needs, starting at the bottom with what he calls deficiency needs: physiological needs such as air, water, food, shelter. Above that in the hierarchy are psychological and social needs such as self-esteem, esteem by others, belongingness, affection, and acceptance. At the top of the hierarchy are moral needs: love, truth, service, justice, perfection, esthetics, meaningfulness.[5]

There is the proposition that reason is only instrumental and cannot serve in the choice of human values, ends, and purposes. That might be defended if life were not better than death, and if health were not preferable to ill health. But given those two propositions, there is an objective basis for a morality serving human needs. Dietitians still do not know all we need to know about what diets are relatively healthful and which are less so. But they do know something about it, and it is not just a matter of subjective preferences. We know that there are conditions that determine the healthfulness of diets, and that we are better off the better we harmonize with these conditions. The same may be said about other aspects of human life. We need to harmonize our conflicting impulses and emotions for our own wholesomeness and health. We need to develop and harmonize our creative potentials with those of other people, or conflicts and suffering may result. Groups of people need to do likewise. And for our economies to be sustainable, we need to harmonize their activities with those of the natural world. It will be self-defeating to harm our life-support system, and it is high time to count depletion of our natural capital as such instead of counting it as income.

Although we are still struggling to know all we need to know about human nature, we know that it provides an objective basis for the good life. We also know that there is not one straight and narrow way that alone will do, but that there are many patterns of life that will work and bring us the maximum benefits. We can also fall short of that in an infinite number of ways, and indeed can make a mess of life instead.

We all know that there is a duality in life's impulses, a nobler and a more debased element, and that we need to cultivate the one and not the other. We all have a conscience, and know guilt when we do not listen to it. Our materialism needs to give way to the old virtues such as prudence, justice, fortitude, and temperance, according to E.F. Schumacher in *Small Is Beautiful*.[6] Virtuous character is still a proper end of humanity. We need a science that treats people as holistic individuals with a structure of human needs and an inborn potential for higher levels of living and more meaningful lives, and we need a culture and polity that promotes that. A science of revealed preference is indeed impoverished.

The good society is one that encourages us in the right directions, that provides the opportunities that everyone needs for personal fulfillment in conjunction with others. The good society promotes community values and the welfare of its members, welfare from biological to cultural, from working conditions to living conditions and consumption. Such sentiments are expressed well by John Hobson in an excellent old book called *Work and Wealth*.[7] The good society grants everyone the right to fair and ample opportunities to develop and harmonize their fine potentialities, and it discourages antisocial activities. It promotes human betterment. The concept of a good society is as old as that of the good life. Both imply an ethical criterion. This vastly transcends simple want satisfaction.

Economics separated itself from its ethical and religious roots after the medieval period. Adam Smith was a professor of moral philosophy, though few students today read his *Theory of Moral Sentiments* in which his conception of human nature is spelled out more fully than in *An Inquiry into the Nature and Causes of the Wealth of Nations*.[8] The latter book is one of political economy. Modern economics has also ceased to be explicitly political, although there is no shortage of explicit political conclusions drawn from its supposedly purely economic analyses.

10. Individual and Social Decision-Making

Economics treats the economy as though it were separate from society, whereas it should be treated as a subsystem of society, polity, and culture. Human preferences are not determined individually but socially. They continually form and reform as people engage in economic activity, according to MIT economist Lester Thurow.[9] The decisions are often large and irreversible, not the small reversible ones assumed by economics. The desire for power is left out of the analysis, yet people struggle for wealth, which is for power, not for future consumption.[10]

Bruno Frey, in *Economics as a Science of Human Behavior,* says that collectives are not decision-makers, but then contends that, at any point in time, human behavior is determined by organizations: the state, interest groups, firms, clubs, families, and so on, while over time by norms, traditions, and laws. And for the society, there are four decision-making systems: pricing in a market system, democracy, hierarchy, and bargaining.[11]

So, are individual actions and social policy governed by ideas, interests, values, emotions, reason, tradition, or culture? Yes, and it is not easy to sort out the relative importance of each with respect to different types of decisions and actions, but it is necessary to make the effort better than does orthodox economics. As Herbert Simon argues, the type of rationality assumed by economists is literally impossible.[12]

Yet orthodox economics has been influential. Witness the famous passage from the *General Theory of Employment, Interest and Money* by John Maynard Keynes: "The ideas of economists and political philosophers, both when they are right and when they are wrong, are more powerful than is commonly understood. Indeed the world is ruled by little else. . . . I am sure that the power of vested interests is vastly exaggerated compared with the gradual encroachments of ideas."[13]

Eduardo Gianetti da Fonseca argues the contrary.[14] He contends that ideas do not rule the world, that passions do. He says that readers and listeners are quite fallible in understanding what they read or hear; they don't get it right. But I contend that, whether right or wrong, it is passionately held ideas that matter and that guide human behavior. And that for the most part these are ideas that are floating around in the culture or are even drummed into us by the subcultures in which we find ourselves.

Demand, Supply, Competition, Invisible Hand

11. Price Determination

Students easily get the impression that the economist's answer to any question is "demand and supply." That is the answer usually given to the question of what determines individual prices. What really completes the answer is, of course, the analysis of what lies behind and determines both demand and supply conditions for different things priced.

Some students may feel there is an elementary difficulty with the demand-and-supply story in that it is stated as though the mechanism operates untouched by human hands. Prices are said to be changed by changes in demand or supply. Of course, prices are set and changed by people as a result of decision-making processes in which people respond to some degree to what they perceive, rightly or wrongly, to be changes in some of the conditions that affect demands and supplies. A human role is recognized in the term "price-makers," though the term "price-takers" seems to suggest absence of human intervention. It is explained that in the latter situation, an individual seller or buyer cannot effectively bargain over price since there are other buyers and sellers ready to complete transactions at a price that has been prevailing in the market. Older textbooks used to illustrate situations in which buyers and sellers could haggle and bargain over price within a range set by what each one was willing to do. In the imaginary perfectly competitive market situation, each side knows, or learns by experience, that the range shrinks to a single price. Apart from the two conditions just mentioned, bargaining and perfect competition, buyers decide whether to buy or not to buy at prices others have set. And the sellers, who are the price-makers (as the term goes, or price-searchers as others would call them), make decisions about prices to charge, based upon their estimates of demand and supply conditions. Presumably they learn by experience that, for any given demand and supply conditions, although they have power to vary price, there is only one price that will maximize their profits. That is how demand and supply, the latter usually implying cost conditions, determine price, not by magic but by human decisions as to prices. Of course, the textbook is talking primarily about equilibrium prices, those that equate quantity demanded and quantity supplied, not primarily about the market prices at any specific time when they may not be at an equilibrium. But even though all prices involve someone's setting them according to some perceived conditions, even the monopolist seems "forced" to set the price that market and cost conditions dictate if the objective is profit maximization.

We are told that prices will be higher in a monopolized or oligopolized market than in a perfectly competitive one. Perhaps they will be higher. But what the textbooks show is that if a perfectly competitive market were to have the innumerable firms collude somehow, or be combined somehow, so that the result was pricing decisions made in terms of a perceived downward sloping demand curve, the resulting prices would be higher than in the perfectly competitive market. It does not follow, however, that any market dominated by a monopoly or oligopoly would have lower prices if the firms were broken up into such small noncolluding units that the market became perfectly competitive. The fact of the matter is that although monopoly or oligopoly may result from collusion or combination, it may also result in or from economies of scale. And to the extent that such economies of scale are present, breaking up productive units into smaller ones would result in higher average costs and higher market prices, not lower prices. The usual propositions about output and misallocation of resources from monopoly and oligopoly are to be thrown out also when scale economies explain market structure. This is obvious in the case of natural monopoly, but sometimes it is not made clear that the possible applicability of scale economies is broader. To be sure, big business structures cannot all be explained as due simply and solely to scale economies.

It seems strange that a firm throwing one more unit of output upon a monopolized market must reduce price to sell it, while if there were many competitors in the market any one firm could sell another unit in the market without lowering the price. The clue to this puzzle is that the analysis assumes that the perfectly competitive market demand is huge relative to the total output of any individual firm, so an added unit of output has a negligible price effect, while for the monopoly, the size of a unit of output of the firm is large relative to the market demand. Thus an output larger than before by one such unit is salable only at a slightly lower price, as indicated by a downward sloping market-demand curve. It is all a matter of the size of the unit of production relative to the total market demand at a given price.

Where there is some degree of market power (monopoly power), a common pricing method is to add some customary markup to costs. This or other such "rules of thumb" may not maximize profits, but is common in the absence of adequate information about marginal costs and marginal revenues. Textbooks generally provide discussions of other pricing methods, including price leadership and the kinked demand curve case, and bargaining. Then, of course, attention should be paid to the various ways in which prices are influenced by government: setting some price minimums and maximums, regulating utility rates, and the like.

A further word is in order here about bargaining power and prices in markets where the amount of competition on the two sides of the market is unequal. It is common knowledge that in labor markets the price paid to hire labor may be much less than would have to be paid were the competition for labor greater than the competition for jobs. This is very significant. Labor unionism is in part a means of trying to improve the bargaining power of some groups of laborers. Clearly the common disparities in bargaining power in labor markets implies the absence of perfect competition, an absence not originating with unionism. Textbooks seldom make all this clear, though job seekers usually find that no single employer needs them as badly as they need a job.

Some textbooks mention the concept of consumers' surplus. They talk nonsense when a demand curve is extended back to the vertical axis, as though it had any real meaning there. What we really know about demand-and-supply curves for anything is confined to a very narrow range of prices and quantities, and even that may be gummed up because the observations may include shifts of either or both curves. Of course, there is no harm in extending these curves somewhat because there is good reason to suppose that they have the same shapes beyond the observed ranges. However, it is not sensible to extend the curves the whole way back to the vertical axis. We never know what somebody would be willing to pay for it if there was only a single unit of the product produced, even one per unit of time. It was nonsense to suppose that one could measure a consumers' surplus under a demand curve drawn clear back to the vertical axis. (Similarly for supply: It is not realistic to assume that a firm would produce a single unit of something at the price shown by extending the supply curve back to the vertical axis.)

Let us review a bit the analysis of price and output determination by a normal downward sloping supply curve and a normal upward sloping supply curve. Is this the general case as we may suppose, or when does it not suffice? Let us recognize first that in reality there is no empirical evidence of what demand or supply quantities would be outside of a relatively small range, and even within this range, either demand or supply may have changed to give the observed result. Of course, we think we are warranted in extending the curves somewhat beyond an observed range.

The firm in perfect competition does not have a normal downward sloping demand curve but has a horizontal demand curve. The normal demand-and-supply curves may be applicable to a perfectly competitive industry in the short run. In the long run its supply curve might be expected to be horizontal. For a monopoly, the demand curve has the normal shape, but it has no normal supply curve as a simple function of price. The quantity supplied is determined not by price but by the position and shape of the marginal revenue curve. For monopoly, both price and quantity are dependent variables, though the cost conditions and the demand conditions are often treated as independent variables. That ceases to be the case when advertising has any effect on the demand curve as well as on costs.

Most firms are neither perfectly competitive nor absolute or natural monopolies, but most have downward sloping demand curves influenced by advertising and hence no simple supply curves as functions of price. If one defines an industry composed of such firms, both its price and the quantity supplied are the result of guesses by member firms as to what they can sell at what price and cost with what advertising outlay. Price is not an independent variable with quantities demanded and supplies dependent, nor are demand-and-supply conditions entirely independent of each other. The further complication is that in reality we generally need to talk about multiple-product firms, some things being joint products. Cost curves for individual products are often hard to know accurately.

Oligopolies introduce another complication to the demand curves. They still slope downward, but the position of a firm's demand curve depends on the reactions expected by other firms to any strategy by any oligopolist. Demand is represented not by a single demand curve but at least by a complex matrix.

Those simple downward sloping demand curves and upward sloping supply curves, drawn with price as an independent variable and quantities as the dependent variables, seem not to be very widely explanatory after all. Prices and quantities demanded and supplied by firms or industries are much more complicated dependent variables, especially when the determining variables are somewhat interdependent. When economics is realistic, it is not simple.

12. Elasticities of Demand and Supply

Economists' favorite way of explaining whether some change produces one result rather than another is to say simply that it depends on some elasticities, usually of demand and supply. They provide a formula for computing elasticities if one has the necessary data on how much people respond to a change in some price or income. Then they show that the outcome of a postulated change will be one thing, given one elasticity, and how it will differ if the elasticity is sufficiently different. The outcome of a price change, in terms of total expenditure on a product, may be shown to be different, not just in degree but in direction, if the demand elasticity is greater than one instead of less than one.

This seems to have made a big contribution to our understanding, but in fact, if no knowledge has been provided as to what the elasticity is in a given situation, it has merely told us that we don't know anything about the outcome. It has dodged the issue rather than having explained something, although it may sound like a valuable explanation of what determines the outcome of an action. But one has only given a name to something, not a real explanation of what will happen if a price changes. To say that the outcome of some change in a situation depends upon elasticities is merely to say that it depends upon how much people respond to that change. Of course it does. But the economist has not added to our knowledge of the outcome unless there is knowledge given or available as to how much that response is going to be or is likely to be for the matter in question. One has not learned as much as one may think if one has merely learned that outcomes depend upon the unknown magnitudes of responses, even though one has learned how to compute numerical values for the concept. If one knows the elasticity in some case, it does not refer to a causal factor that explains people's behavior; it is only a convenient shorthand name for the amount of behavior response.

13. Market Prices and Social Values

A basic question is whether prices in the market represent social values properly. Market prices are in a sense social valuations, reflective of people's demands and the relative scarcities of the resources required to respond to those demands. Economists critical of government-control-led prices speak of competitive market prices as scarcity prices, imply-ing that they represent true social valuations. Then they admit that some social valuations are not adequately represented in even perfectly com-petitive markets, let alone in actual markets. What are called "externali-ties" are admittedly not registered in markets. These include the values of what are termed "public goods." Of course, all sorts of social bene-fits and costs are external to the producing firms.

There is the old quip that some people know the price of everything but the value of nothing. Living should tell anyone that there are many values in life that the market does not register at all or registers wrongly. Therefore in individual lives and in social policy we not only should, but actually must, second-guess the market on some relative values. So it is not being objective, and value-judgment-free, to accept market values as true social values.

To be sure, the search for standards of social value is a baffling task, but a very important and necessary one. There is no yardstick as sim-ple as dollar prices. But there is no real basis for objecting to doing something to alter the resource allocation that the market would give us if we really could and did follow that alone.

Of course, a case has to be made to alter the resource allocations that market prices would yield, and we do so quite readily in some areas. For example, we make some activities illegal rather than letting them be promoted by the values that the market would put on them. We even deliberately tax some things to reduce use, and we subsidize other things because we judge the market valuation to be erroneous and not in the social interest.

Despite all the virtues economists legitimately allege for a market system and market pricing, there is ample room and reason for social policy to second-guess the market in some instances where a case can be made that social values are different from market prices. Economists who try to have the last word on the matter by alleging an objective basis for criticizing any departure from market pricing are on unsound ground. To approve of market valuations entirely would imply approving of a situation where some people work full-time and still are in poverty, and few people really approve of that. In addition, if market valuations alone were to determine resource allocation, there would be no government services. All roads would be toll roads, there would be no national defense, only private police and fire departments, and justice would be paid for through private courts. Anarchism, real libertarianism, would prevail.

Indeed if market prices were to represent all social values in any fashion, let alone properly, all private activities that now do not go through the market would have to do so and be bought and sold. We would have to buy and sell spouses and children. All volunteer activity would have to be bought and sold. Everything people did would have to involve buying and selling. All this is, of course, absurd, undesirable, and even impossible. But it tells us clearly that the markets' pricing is only a subset of the set of social values, and not always an accurate subset at that. Virtuous or creative persons have no market price, but their social value is great. The case rests.

Market prices are very useful indeed, but they simply cannot properly represent all social values, and so there is always room to second-guess market prices in terms of a set of social values. The further problem is that people's notions differ as to what are proper social valuations. That is so even in relatively homogeneous cultures, let alone in cases of cultural pluralism and heterogeneity. It can be argued that market prices are as far as we can go, practically speaking. But that is not true because substantial majorities would be found on some issues, as for instance the failure of markets to price properly the services of the working poor. Indeed a substantial majority are not anarchists and do not want services now provided by government to be dependent on the market pricing of them. Whenever there is enough public sentiment for interference with market prices, it is clear that social values differ from market prices. Economists should take note, not argue that it is all a mistake or uneconomic or inefficient.

The final relevant argument will be discussed further later, but needs to be mentioned here before we go on. Prices are obviously affected by demand, and the demand of everyone is not equal—when incomes are highly unequal, some people stuff the ballot box in voting for what they want resources used for. The market says it is efficient to provide luxuries for the rich, but sometimes not efficient to meet the more urgent needs of the poor.

14. The Perfect Competition Norm

The textbook treatments of markets usually begin with the assumption that they are perfectly competitive and work out a perfectly competitive equilibrium. The assumption is not in accord with the facts, since oligopolies dominate, and we are not dealing with a closed determinate mechanical system. Our actual observations are always of disequilibrium, and the kaleidoscopic character of economic relationships makes the course of economic affairs a limitless and often unique series of historical facts.[15]

Yet one might well gather from many an economic principles textbook that perfect competition is a sort of norm, which might be taken to imply that any departures from perfect competition are generally unfortunate. Indeed the case is made for a perfectly competitive market structure as a norm by analyses purporting to show that it alone provides maximum allocative efficiency. It is also said to guarantee what may be called technical or productive efficiency because the inefficient firms would have higher costs and would fail. All this might be taken as providing the rationale for measures such as antitrust legislation to enforce competition, although at most they only place limits on some moves "too far" away from the norm, except of course in the case of natural monopoly that has to be accepted. Actually the case for maintaining rather highly competitive structures and practices does not depend upon whether perfect competition is a proper norm or not.

The suggestion here is that perfect competition should not be considered the social norm. The usual textbook analysis that demonstrates the efficiency of perfect competition in equilibrium in a static model is logically correct. But the model abstracts from some human considerations that are important in the actual world. Perfect competition does not overcome the difficulty already noted in connection with price determination that even competitive prices are not always correctly representative of social value, so if a norm it would be subject to such *major* qualifications and shortcomings.

There is such a thing as excessive or cutthroat competition, and though that is usually associated with oligopoly, the more real the competition the greater the pressure to lower costs, and lowering costs may drive a whole industry to sacrifice product quality, working conditions, and the environment. According to the standard analysis of perfect competition, its return on capital tends toward the minimum necessary to obtain and keep the capital in each such perfectly competitive industry. Practically speaking, that means that the funds for research and development upon which we depend for much technological change and other innovations would be zero.

Besides, whatever might be true of an equilibrium situation, in the real world of rather rapid economic change, we are virtually never in equilibrium but are constantly chasing the ever moving equilibrium targets. Rapid change requires a high degree of mobility of resources, including labor, especially if the economy is a perfectly competitive one. Whatever may be said about substantial short-run skill mobility, people do not thrive, nor do social conditions improve, with a high degree of geographical mobility of labor. Indeed the areas in our cities that display the most human mobility to keep up with economic change requirements have the highest rates of personal and social disorganization. Human beings need community roots, not perfect mobility. As for skill mobility, it is unrealistic to expect it to be very rapid for many people; besides which, so much economic insecurity and dumping of people on scrap heaps if they don't or can't retool upon demand is undesirable. This sounds like a case against too rapid change, and it is; but it is not a case for a cartelized economy. It is a statement that perfect competition, if indeed possible, is humanly harsher than a more moderated degree of competition, for which a better case can be made. There may be some other aspects of the concept that are not normative that may be discussed along with questions of possibility and even conceivability.

There is the question of whether perfect competition as a concept makes sense for an industry and for an economy, and whether it is even possible. It seems such a simple concept and is so useful for pedagogical purposes, but one needs to examine the list of conditions that are stated as defining perfect competition. Some of them raise no problems of possibility or conceptual sense. For example, it is not too unrealistic or too difficult to imagine a situation for an industry (but not for every part of the whole economy) in which the numbers of buyers and sellers are both so large that each is likely as a practical matter to perceive its own influence on the market price to be negligible. But in fact there are economies of scale in some lines of production that do not always stop with firms so small relative to market demand. (There are even what are called natural monopolies.) So in this respect, at least, a perfectly competitive economy is impossible. There could be no equilibrium where such economies were not realized if they were possible. But moreover, it would not be better to avoid those scale economies rather than take advantage of them, so perfect competition would not be normative, as well as not providing a possible equilibrium.

Another requirement for perfect competition is product homogeneity in each industry. Can it be argued that it would be possible? It certainly would not be considered desirable to have so much standardization as to eliminate all product differentiation. Can you imagine each product variation to have so many producers and consumers that none could expect to influence price at all? Perhaps substitutability among differentiated products would be enough for that result, but do we not then have a type of monopolistic competition rather than meeting the efficiency norm claimed for perfect competition?

Perfect competition involves perfect price flexibility, another supposed normative aspect of it. That eliminates fixed contracts and fixed debts. Would everything work so well if none were fixed? What would then prevent more severe cumulative spirals up or down in price levels than we have had? And if some prices, debts, and contracts are fixed, while current prices are completely flexible, real price deflation can be absolutely ruinous, bankrupting many otherwise sound economic operations. The argument does not call for complete price rigidity, it calls for more sophistication about the possibility and desirability of partial or total perfect price flexibility.

Perfect competition is ordinarily conceived as entailing free entry and exit from any industry, "free" meaning completely unrestricted entry and exit, without any obstacle thereto. Is it really conceivable that this could be the case for firms that require tremendous investments in real capital as well as money capital? Or is the norm supposed to be an economy in which scale economies stop before such scale is reached?

And what about the possibility of perfect resource mobility in a world of fairly rapid change? We can at least conceive of rapid geographical mobility of labor, but have already argued its undesirability, and have suggested the undesirability as well as impossibility of perfect short-run skill mobility. And although liquid capital can be about as mobile as one can conceive, disinvestment of embodied productive capital is almost always very slow and indeed sometimes impossible. There is zero mobility of some embodied capital when change prevents one from getting some of one's money capital out and inflicts a real capital loss.

Finally, there is the matter of the degree of knowledge assumed to be required for perfect competition to do all that is claimed for it in the model. All market participants are, in the typical model, assumed to have complete and correct information about everything relevant to their economic decisions. That would be a difficult condition to meet even in a static model, and when one thinks of what is entailed in a dynamic situation, the condition is clearly impossible to meet. What is relevant and assumed known includes future magnitudes that cannot really be known because no one can know the future. The perfect competitor makes decisions assuming he has no effect upon those magnitudes. But they are affected in part by the decisions made by all the firm's competitors in the present, each one assuming it has no effect. It appears that each makes decisions based on future values that their own actions make wrong.

It is not surprising that no economy is perfectly competitive because it is difficult to imagine all the conditions for perfect competition being met. It is surprising that textbooks sometimes give the impression that perfect competition provides a norm against which economies should be judged. A perfectly competitive economy is undesirable in some respects, impossible in some, and even inconceivable in some.

Could the same be said of any single industry in at least some of the specific respects already discussed? If so, that is because the perfect competition concept is a sort of extreme concept. There is such a thing as "workable competition" that is inherently compatible with some conceivable and feasible norms. Perhaps more attention should be paid to such a concept and its normative features, with special attention to the reasons that perfect competition is not normative.

15. The Invisible Hand

Adam Smith's concept of the invisible hand is still very visible in economics books and in the ideology of laissez-faire political-economic conservatism. The idea is that a competitive market will allocate resources according to consumer demand, the self-interest of producers being made by the invisible hand of the market to serve consumer interests more reliably than dependence on producer beneficence. No one ever supposed that producer beneficence could supply public needs. But a careful reading of Adam Smith would emphasize the importance of competition in the market, and indeed the necessity of efforts to maintain competition in the face of the alleged tendency of businessmen to use even luncheon meetings to hatch plots at the expense of the consumer.

This claim that the market's invisible hand serves consumer interest requires discussion both pro and con. It is to a large extent true, and that is of tremendous importance. No comparable claim can be made generally for any alternative. The competitive market is the most economical and least bureaucratic way of doing the meritorious things it does. Serving consumer interests is generally regarded as of such great importance that the efficiency of a market-type economy is often stated in terms of how well it serves the consumer.

That is all true to a large and very significant extent. But it is not the whole truth. It is also true that in a market-dominated economy, "crime" in the market still pays at times, and indeed all too often. "Crime" is in quotation marks because the concept here is not a legal one. Here attention is being called to the virtually universal knowledge of, and often the experience of, practices on the part of business that either harm consumers, or at the least, result in business's making profit out of practices that serve the consumer less well than would be both possible and much preferable to the consumer. The consumer is often not well served, and in that sense exceptions to the claims made for the invisible hand abound. In the light of the claims, actual harm to consumers could be considered a sort of crime. In some cases such harm has been made a legal crime. The potential forms of "disservice" to consumers, often deliberate since it is perceived as more profitable than better service to them, are virtually innumerable, so an attempt at a thoroughgoing legislative solution would result in a cure that might be worse than the disease it would be designed to cure.

The fact is that markets necessarily do depend upon a culture-determined morality to work at all, since it would be impossible to spell out in written contracts everything involved in every economic transaction. A great deal of business is necessarily done with a large degree of trust, although the legal profession is able to thrive well, in part because the trust is sometimes not warranted. But, fortunately for everybody, there are many things that most businesspeople would not do just to gain economically. Whether the moral standards in the marketplace are lower or higher than at some earlier period in history is debatable. The old "caveat emptor" slogan would not be as readily defended as necessary for consumers generally, or indeed expressed as an appropriate stance for business now, as it used to be. But clearly there is still much room for improvement in business morality in markets. And despite the degree of validity in the correctly claimed advantages of markets, the social choices will remain: continued shortcomings in consumer service, improved business morality, attempts at legislative remedies, or some combination of these. Certainly consumer education, some additional consumer protective legislation, and a substantial improvement in business morality would all be needed to make the market system serve the consumer anywhere nearly as well as the claims for the invisible hand suggest. The question is why economics textbooks do not explore this issue in depth instead of being content with praise of the market system, praise that may be deserved but that needs the qualification that much improvement would still be warranted.

Indeed one may question why business does not seem to conceive that it could gain as much or more by obtaining better feedback from consumers than from other types of market surveys. Salespeople get a lot of feedback from customers, but that is where most of it stops rather than being fed back up the line and influencing the producer. Consumer sovereignty presumably would be much improved, for consumer freedom to buy or not buy can provide only limited feedback when consumer alternatives are limited, as is necessarily the case.

There is an even more fundamental challenge to the claims made for the invisible hand. The claims assume that the market serves consumer demands that are independent of the market. Economists do not inquire into the origins of consumer demands; so far as economics is concerned, they are immaculately conceived. That leaves it to sociologists or somebody else to describe their cultural origins and changes. But what if the demands the market is said to serve so well are themselves the product of the operations of businesses that then brag about how well they serve the demands? John Kenneth Galbraith has put it bluntly in suggesting that a squirrel cage is a dubious model for how to make an economy prosper, let alone for bragging about how well the squirrel is served. And who can deny that in our economy we are simply swamped with advertising designed to make us keep the cage rotating? Of course, advertising is necessary to enable consumers to know what is available where and at what prices. But clearly most advertising is not for the purpose, and does not serve well the purpose, of enabling consumers to purchase wisely. Indeed all too much of it has sunk to the morality of trying to treat consumers like Pavlov's dog and make us water at the mouth for the advertised product. To the degree that such advertising is successful, the economy becomes the squirrel cage, and the claim made for the invisible hand is seriously erroneous. Fortunately our natural skepticism prevents total brainwashing by advertisers, but clearly much of their effort is subversive of the sort of economy that is defensible in invisible-hand terms.

There is one very important qualification of the criticism just made. Not all production is either a response to some exogenously determined consumer demand or to demand conditioned or heavily influenced by advertising. One of the truly remarkable things about our American economy is the extent to which Americans are innovators. New products, or improvements on old products, are being introduced into the market all the time. There was no previous demand evident, but some people saw the possibility that people would want these products if they were available. One way or another, the finances and production facilities were obtained and the new products were produced, advertised, and offered to the market. Many are the products of research and development in established firms, but not all are. Not all of them turn out to be good bets or improve human well-being, but a very large number of them do because they represent either something new and desirable or something that is a real improvement on what was previously available. So it is that almost every conceivable manual operation in production itself now has a specialized machine to aid the production process. Many of these innovations have increased human productivity tremendously. Just compare many American production methods with those of a hundred years ago here, or those now prevailing in many less developed countries. It is hard to exaggerate the importance of innovation for any economy. We can properly brag about our rate of innovation.

This is the place to explore another aspect of the legitimate defense of markets along with some implications that are generally neglected because uncomfortable qualifications arise in practice. In a broad sense, the basic problem of social organization is to structure relations between people and between groups so that both sides win in their relationships with one another instead of one winning and one losing. Communists have often claimed that in markets one side loses what the other side gains. The rebuttal is that in a system of free contract, both parties to the transaction gain. The rebuttal can be correct, although it depends upon certain conditions being met, and it leaves open the question of whether the division of the gains is equitable.

Clearly if each side knows exactly what it is doing when it enters into an economic transaction, knows what its alternatives are, and indeed has comparable and viable alternatives rather than being forced to enter the transaction, either each side will gain or the transaction will not take place. Economist Frank Knight used to summarize this in class by saying that both sides benefit when the relation is free of force and fraud, for only then is it truly free contract.

The terms "force" and "fraud" are neat summaries, but require some elucidation. And it turns out that the conditions are not always met and sometimes not even very closely approximated for the full implications of freedom to be applicable. Force does not necessarily mean that one has a gun at one's head to sign a contract. There is such a thing as being under more or less duress to accept terms that are not those one would willingly and freely accept if not under some type of pressure to accept them. A good illustration is the situation of the unemployed worker being offered employment terms that are not those he would freely accept if he were not in great need of a job and unable to find a satisfactory one. It turns out that true freedom is a matter of having comparable and viable alternatives and that one knows about them. Otherwise one is under some degree of duress and hence not fully free.

As for the term "fraud," it has connotations that are appropriate at times, but can imply something short of what is ordinarily considered outright fraud. The condition for free contract is that one knows every-

thing relevant before entering the contract, not simply enough to prevent being completely defrauded. One will not knowingly enter into a
transaction if there is another which would be more beneficial, for
although there might not be an absolute loss, one would nonetheless
lose a greater benefit that one would not knowingly and willingly lose.
Again the case is made for informative advertising as essential if the
claims for free contract are to be validated. Much advertising does not
meet the test, for it is either uninformative or misleading or an irrelevant emotional appeal or outright emotional conditioning. The subver-
siveness of such advertising needs to be seen through by the victims
and its intended effects on us need to be negated. A common defense
of advertising that tries to subvert instead of serve the consumer is that
it works. There is evidence that it does influence consumers. People
trained in psychology have applied their knowledge to manipulate
other people through advertising, although it is not often as successful
as the buyers of the advertising hope. The point that needs to be made
here is that the test of an action is not simply its workability, but its
morality as well. Hitler's gas chambers also worked. It is immoral to
treat consumers like Pavlov's dog, even if they did not have to pay for
such treatment. Unfortunately they cannot avoid paying to be thus
maltreated because the advertising cost is added to the prices of the
products. It is simply not true that our economy would not work if it
were not for the barrage of advertising of the types being criticized
here. To be sure, consumer markets would be somewhat different,
some things would be less profitable and other things more profitable.
And the claims made for the mutuality from market transactions could
be defended much more honestly because true freedom of contract
would have more real meaning, people would know exactly what they
were getting—with no fraudulent claims to even try to delude them.

As a broad generalization, it may be contended that between any
two individuals, between any two groups, and between the individual
and the group, there is both potential mutual benefit and potential
conflict of interest. The competitive market, when the above-discussed
conditions are met, is a social institution that effectuates (via the invisible hand) the potential mutuality between the individual and the group
(in one case between the producer and consumers). The potential conflict lies in the division between producer and consumer of the gains
from their joint transactions. Consensus on a concept of equity in the
division of gains can alone resolve the conflict. Would any questions

be raised if it could be shown that 95 percent of the gain went to the producers' side and 5 percent to the consumers' side, or would there be equal concern if the percentages were reversed? Should any consideration be given to how much of the gain was needed as an incentive to producers to bring the products to market? Broader aspects of the income distribution issue will be discussed later. Markets certainly operate differently with different distributions of income. High incomes stuff the market ballot box. And sizable differentials in economic power, about which something has already been said, arise from sizable inequalities of income and wealth.

It is quite conceivable that both parties to a transaction may gain from it, even equitably, but that third parties may suffer. That is the case when external costs are inflicted upon them. To be sure, they may benefit if there are external benefits. The latter are no problem. We might hope that there are many instances of private economic transactions as well as public policies from which everyone affected benefits. But we know that is not always the case, and we should inquire as to how common external costs are, and what, if anything, can be done about them. The claim is often made that the entire public generally benefits from a market economy, not just the parties to each transaction. Can conditions be determined that will conduce to more general public benefits from market operations, that is, benefits to third parties generally?

There are some additional conditions that need to be met for a so-called market system economy and its invisible hand to operate optimally and meet the various claims made for it. Economic conditions include adequate competition and a combination of a work ethic and sufficient economic incentive for everyone. The personal qualities needed include plenty of simple honesty, initiative, innovativeness, adaptability, and a variety of skills including entrepreneurial and managerial skills. Political conditions include political stability, a framework of law defining rights and responsibilities, penalties for antisocial conduct, contract law, property law, bankruptcy law, and so on. Even cultural heritage may be helpful or not, as markets work differently in different cultural settings. Saying all this does not specify the specific content of each of these conditions, and about that much argument necessarily arises.

A market system is obviously a system that entails very extensive economic interdependence. Adam Smith's classic economic analysis made more of the gains from specialization, division of labor, and thence of exchange than of the words "invisible hand." The productivity made possible by the interdependence described can hardly be exaggerated, for self-sufficient producers simply could not have produced modern standards of living. But the insecurities from interdependence in the face of economic change need to be spoken of in the same breath. And when the insecurities are discussed, it is desirable to consider the ways in which various insecurities can also be better dealt with through interdependence than without it. Both individual and social insurance are such methods.

The invisible-hand analysis is an instance of economics serving as apologetics for the market economies. The defense of market systems establishes a norm, but the norm is not really identical, for reasons already given, with any actual market economy. The norm is sometimes stated in terms of an achievable equilibrium. An actual market never achieves an equilibrium; it is always chasing one but never reaching it. It never reaches it because the conditions change and change the equilibrium before adjustments to previous changes in conditions are complete. And the adjustments depend in part on the set of economic institutions prevailing. Indeed we cannot even specify the nature of the adjustment scientifically because of the troublesome element of free will.[16]

It is indeed appropriate that economics evaluates economic arrangements in terms of a norm of efficient allocation of social resources, though the complexity and uniqueness of situations frustrate efforts to give practical advice instead of abstract generalizations.[17] The question is which economic institutions are desirable along with the market. The assumption sometimes made that institutions evolve into their most efficient form precludes consideration of institutional reform. The old concept of cultural lag would introduce a more realistic assumption. There is every reason to study the institutional frameworks of different markets in an economy and the different institutional frameworks in different economies to see what differences they make in the operation of markets.

One institution, of course, is government. Government is involved in market-dominated economies in several ways not discussed here. One is through providing the legal framework in which markets operate. One is through the government sector of the economy as an alternative to some markets. And another is regulating in various ways the operation of markets. Markets are sometimes constrained by governments. There is no such thing as a market operating without constraints, including various traditional, moral, and legal constraints. Debate continues on what are legitimate constraints on economic activity in the market.[18] Society is clearly the interested party in what the constraints should be. The basic question is, how can the game be made fair? Fair both in its processes and indeed in its outcomes? Even economists should give some careful consideration to such issues if anything they say is to be taken seriously.

Money and Finance

16. The Influence and Safety of Finance

The old saying is that it takes money to make money. Indeed to make anything by modern production methods requires ample funds. So being in a position to dole out funds on any terms gives the holders of the funds great economic power and influence. What gets produced and what does not is in large measure determined by the ability or inability to finance their production. So who holds loanable funds, and their ways of deciding who gets them, has tremendous economic importance. It is not hard to explain why fine office buildings and luxury apartments get built but not low-cost housing. Those with loanable funds do not gain or gain as much by financing the latter.

Much loanable finance comes from savings. The rich save more than others. Business also saves, usually with an intended use in mind. Credit creation also adds to available finance. Much of the financing of economic operations is done through various financial institutions. Textbooks usually describe this adequately.

Economics has much to do with the efficient allocation of resources, which is to say their use in the production of the greatest market value. Over time the increase in productivity depends heavily, but not exclusively, upon the resources allocated to research and development, to improved technologies, and to increases in the capital-to-labor ratio. This involves allocation of investable funds and is presumably based indirectly on expected consumer demand in markets, business demand, and demand by governments.

The textbooks would have it that all market allocations of resources are performed by the price mechanism, relative prices reflecting underlying demand and supply conditions. The interest rate is designated as the price that allocates finance, and thus also resources, by eliminating those projects whose yields are not expected to cover the interest rate and required profit rate. In the aggregate, financial institutions as holders or creators of loanable funds certainly influence the allocation of resources. How they allocate them is said to be determined by the interest rate, meaning, of course, the pattern of interest rates, since the prices to borrow or lend funds depend upon a variety of things such as the length of the loan, the purpose, the security for the lender, judgments as to risk, and bargaining power or competition.

What needs to be added explicitly is that the allocation of loanable funds (and hence of some resources) depends also upon the pattern of financial institutions. This is itself only in part a reflection of the prices obtainable for different types of loans. The highly developed system of financial institutions in this country is, to be sure, based on the fact that it became profitable for some institutions to specialize in one or only a few types of financial instruments. A commercial paper house, for example, is not the sort of department store of finance that a commercial bank is. But in the fields of agricultural credit and real estate credit, the market's financial institutions were alleged not to provide fair and adequate access to loanable funds, and that led to two whole sets of federally established financial institutions in those fields. Although these institutions largely mobilized private, not government, funds, the allocation of funds to those two sectors of the economy increased substantially as a result.

So it needs to be said that the allocation of loanable funds, and hence of resources, is determined not only by the pattern of interest rates but also by the pattern of financial institutions.

Can anything be said about the merits of the resulting allocation of loanable funds? By what criteria should it be judged, and, if lacking in any respect, by what means might it be improved? The deliberate establishment of financial institutions to serve certain economic sectors that were judged not to be receiving a fair and adequate share of funds illustrates both a criterion and a remedy already used. Note that until some recent difficulties arose that require special explanation, especially the savings-and-loan fiasco, the institutions that developed or were established operated profitably in the market without continuous subsidy.

Presumably each financial institution allocates its funds wherever it can get the highest expected rate of return, while taking risk into account, within the area in which it specializes to some degree. And the funds it can attract to lend depend also upon that rate, for that rate determines the rates it can offer.

The usual story is that the economic sectors where funds are most needed will be able to pay the highest rates and will thereby attract the most funds. But it seems as though the sectors of the greatest need in some sense are those that can pay least and are therefore starved for funds. Under competitive pressures from foreign steel producers, the American steel industry needed funds to modernize. But the very fact that it needed funds prevented it from getting them, since the rate of return on its stock was low, a reflection of competition and the need to attract capital to modernize. One could say that the stock market was telling us that the American steel industry should close shop and our loanable funds should be invested wherever they could get a higher return. However, it is not entirely clear that it would have provided the most productive future for our country if America had lost its steel industry rather than finding ways to finance the modernizing of it.

The stock market may not be an entirely trustworthy guide to where funds should be allocated. Yet its mere existence is important for raising funds for various purposes. Who would invest in financial securities if there were not such a ready market in which to resell them if one unexpectedly needed one's money back? To be sure, there is no guarantee that one will get back as much as one invested. But the gambling "instinct" in many people is strong enough that they take that risk in the hope of making a capital gain. Indeed the stock market may be dominated by speculators hoping for capital gains from reselling securities for more than they paid for them.

The influence of the stock market on the availability of finance also has a pernicious influence on the time horizon of business; namely, it often makes short-run profit considerations outweigh those that might better dominate but that would pay off only further in the future. There is a great deal of pressure now on large numbers of businesses whose stock is listed on stock exchanges to cut costs one way or another to boost the short-run price of their stock, quite without regard to the long-run consequences of such business actions.

That our whole system of financial institutions needs some rethinking is obvious enough in recent years, though neither the textbooks nor the popular ideology are very helpful in provoking sufficient rethinking of the issues. For a time we even had farmers being pushed into borrowing more than long-run considerations warranted, the lenders judging on the basis of unusually high grain prices and farmers' equity in overpriced farmland, but not on the basis of reasonable expectations regarding future farm income.

Then we had rising interest rates caused by inflation creating problems for savings and loans. The remedy, like that suggested since then for commercial banks, was to improve their profits by extending their powers into competitive fields in which they had little experience. That along with deregulation, which became a religion that did not discriminate adequately between what made sense and what did not, resulted in more failures. It should not surprise us that corruption replaced good business, and that friends and white elephants were financed, from which there was very little solid prospect of repayment.

We are told since then that we must limit deposit insurance and thus restore "market discipline" to keep banks and thrifts sound—as though depositors, even large ones, could know more about a financial institution's riskiness than can professional bank examiners. And when depositors react on the basis of rumors, we have restored not soundness but a type of instability into the financial system that deposit insurance was supposed to end. Of course, even recessions will occur, but a financial system needs to be able to withstand them without creating credit crises. For that a knowledgeable central bank like our Federal Reserve System, not dominated by profit maximization, is absolutely essential.

It should be entirely obvious that the country needs to keep all its monetary transactions balances perfectly safe, whatever that takes. It should also be clear that people need perfectly safe outlets for at least some portion of their savings, a portion that each person can decide for himself or herself. People most certainly do not want to have their pensions at risk either, nor do they want to find, when they need to rely on their insurance companies, that they have loaded up with junk bonds or for any other reason have gone bankrupt. There is a dearth of leadership rethinking how to keep these institutions safer. Let students be stimulated to learn what they need to learn to contribute to solutions to these problems instead of being content to learn textbook theories and acceptance of the status quo.

It should be obvious that some financial institutions cannot both be protected, as people need them to be, and at the same time earn rates competitive with those offered by other financial institutions that take on more risky ventures. Where safety and liquidity are needed (for transaction balances in commercial banks), and where safety and solvency are needed (for pensions and insurance), there is no way they can be provided by junk bond investments or other risky new financial products. For the purposes indicated, restrictions of the relevant financial institutions to government securities or to new forms of securitization that are tied to the long-run general profitability of the economy are the sort of answer we should be considering. Of course people can take whatever risks they want in search of higher potential returns for any of their funds they are not as dependent on, and on which they don't get and should not get any government insurance.

As for Wall Street investment banking, it has been busily trying to get the Japanese to buy out U.S. businesses when it could not get enough other American businesses to take one another over. And at times, the highest expected returns for individuals and institutions with funds to play with appear to be in purely financial speculation. That can hardly be defended as in the best interest of the economy's future. The highest returns would seem in recent years to be in financing various sorts of business takeovers. Clearly some people made lots of money in the game, much more than could be made by producing more real wealth in the same time. Commentators wondered out loud about the future of an economy when students were flocking into finance in the hopes of making their millions quickly in Wall Street, as many did. How efficient an economy is it when it uses a lot of people just in financial manipulations? The public might be better served by their getting into the production end of business and working their way into managing businesses they learn from the ground up. But the allocation of some labor resources is itself directed not by the returns to production but by the lure of fancy returns on financial manipulations. Those who can throw huge sums of money into financial switches that boost stock prices, for the gain of some, often load business with excessive debt. When security speculation (gambling) reaps much higher returns than the needed research and development, which may not follow at all, or follow to a small and less rewarded extent, something seems to be wrong. A big sample of it was reported in *America: What Went Wrong?* by Barlett and Steele.

The question should be raised as to what if anything can be done about the problems, and thus far there appears to be no agreed upon or clear solution. One may ask not simply what is dominating the stock markets, but who is making the decisions that are dominating it in the present fashion, and what could change their incentives in a direction that would be more beneficial. This is not the place to review the whole discussion of the matter, nor can one expect an adequate analysis of the issues in the mass media. Suffice it here to refer to the notion that the securities markets might be improved in one respect if short-term churning of security holdings were discouraged by the tax structure so that most security purchases would be made as expected long-term investments. The problem is how in any case to maintain the liquidity of the financial markets so that those investors needing to get out of them due to their own situation can do so normally without huge capital losses.

It is clear that the decisions of business to seek funds through equities or debt is heavily influenced by the tax structure that allows business to treat interest payments on debt as a cost of production, and thus not taxable, while dividends paid on stock are treated as taxable profit. Of course, at least part of the dividend payments is a cost of obtaining capital just as is interest on debt, though part of dividend payments does constitute profit. The question to start with is what can be said in general about the optimal combination of debt and equity capital for businesses in different situations. Then one can consider what tax structure could best promote instead of distort the desired result. Would the market, if a neutral tax policy in this respect existed, lead to the optimum? Or does the tax structure need to weight the matter in one direction instead of the other? Unless whatever the market does is defined as optimal, the matter is suitable for analysis.

Much criticism of other economies and sometimes of our own by economists has as an underlying premise that markets, at least to the degree that they are competitive, produce optimal results in all respects. Second-guessing the market or altering its results is criticized as inherently inefficient. The matter needs further consideration. Here questions are being raised as to what would define an optimal allocation of loanable funds, whether the way loanable funds are being allocated in our economy now is optimal, whether the only departures from optimality are due to government, and what sorts of changes in the economy could be defended as improving the allocation. In addition, how can we keep funds safe that need to be kept safe, and still maintain liquid markets?

It has generally been assumed that there was no way to help those in poverty by providing them with credit. By all the usual criteria, that was right. Yet in many of the less developed countries, the poor often get credit, but they get it only at such usurious rates of interest that many poor farmers or businesses never succeed in getting out of debt. And then along came the very successful Grameen banks, started initially by just one person who had an idea of how it might be done and who tried it out. He lent a small sum to a group of about a dozen women for a small venture. The group was responsible for repayment of the loan of the borrower. The loan was in fact repaid, and then another member of the group got the loan, on the same terms and with the same result. This showed one way to do it, and now Grameen banks are spreading. The amount of credit thus allocated is very small, but it is highly significant. The question now is whether there is some variant of this idea that would work in America. We badly need to revitalize the decaying parts of our central cities. The need is great. The risk is high but the probable rate of return for a lender is very low. Is there any way to meet the need when there are high returns that beckon elsewhere? We need to put our brains to such problems and try some things. Habitat for Humanity has found a way to build houses for the poor where none of the usual financial inducements existed. It works! Are there any in the class who want to tackle any of the real problems that our country and our world face and seem incapable of dealing with? Some of them lie in the world of finance. Wall Street is not interested. It is busy wearing out those who are busy trying to make money fast.

The Business Firm
and Society

17. The Firm and Profit Maximization

The typical textbook treatment of the economics of the firm is fine as a beginning, but is only a beginning and not the place to stop. It is a start to think of the firm in different market situations as knowing something about its demand curve and its cost curves and hence finding profit maximization to be quite simple. Indeed it has the merit of being prescriptive and telling a firm desiring to maximize profit what is required in a simple situation.

But few business firms produce only a single product or service, and many sell in more than one market. The analysis of price discrimination by a monopolist shows how profit can be maximized by charging different prices in markets with different known demand elasticities. In principle, multiple products may be handled by comparing marginal revenues and marginal costs for each product singly; but there are some problems in connection with short-run fixed costs that are variable only in the long run, and joint costs of two or more products are troublesome even in the short run. Even when the textbook deals with these matters with such models as we have, it has not finished the job. The models are more prescriptive than descriptive; they tell how to maximize profit, given certain information. That may have its uses.

But the models are not generally a description of what is going on in the business world, or why. The analysis needs at least to be extended to deal with the considerations introduced by uncertainties to which we have alluded above, and then deal with other realities of the world of business. One would not recognize that one is talking about the same world if one reads the textbook theory of the firm and then reads such publications as *Business Week* magazine. The writers for *Business Week* speak at length of the extent to which firms are concerned about their changing market positions or about their rates of growth, and then talk of the apparent or announced strategies of the firms to deal with these as their major problems.

Indeed one can come away from reading *Business Week* with a serious question as to whether profit maximization is the name of the game that business firms are playing. On the basis of the textbook, one would expect to read in article after article that the strategies employed by firm after firm were chosen because they were confidently expected to increase profits. Instead one reads week after week that firms' strategies appear to be responses to concern over the rate of growth, or over loss of market share, or to be efforts to increase growth or market share. Of course, one may postulate that growth or market share and profit maximization are highly if not perfectly correlated, but there is room to doubt that the motivation question is thereby resolved, whatever the correlation. Without doubt, firms that do not make profit at all do not last indefinitely. But that does not mean that firms' first concern is profit maximization. The motivation may be just growth or market share to puff up the ego of the CEO.

Where the press reports profit changes, as in market sections of the newspapers, the concern is stock prices. It should be obvious that those prices are a function of differences of opinion among not too well informed speculators. Profits are taken into account, but mainly as a matter of whether the reported profits are greater or less than the speculators had predicted.

Concern with other stakeholders is little reported and stock speculators have no interest in the matter except when such concern has clearly reduced profits. Then they are irate and demand cost reductions.

A direct study of the decision-making process in firms would seem to be in order, and discussion of such matters should be added to the theory of the firm. The decision-making structure in firms of different sizes is the place to start this part of the empirical study of firms and profit maximization. Then there is the question as to the motivation structures of the decision-makers. And finally, what is the incentive structure? The "culture" of the business community needs direct study. Putting these things together, one would be in a position to say something about profit maximization and about other values pursued in business decisions.

It rather appears as though the dominant motivation for many business decisions is the desire of some decision-maker to enhance his or her own status. This should not be too surprising, because at least some minimum status seems to be important to everyone, and it is evident that for some people a high relative status is of paramount importance. In the world of big business, at least, status in the eyes of big business leaders is conferred above all by the size of the business that one in some sense heads. Hence growth of a firm may be the main objective of the business leader, and though it may be possible only if profits are expected to permit, it is not necessarily true that the decision to grow is primarily or at all a decision to try to maximize profit. The business analog of keeping up with the Joneses is maintaining market share, and gaining market share is the analog of getting ahead of the Joneses, and that really is gaining status in the community, in this case in both the business community and the wider community.

The whole wave of buyouts, takeovers, and mergers, when it involves loading a company with debt, is not obviously explicable just in terms of profit maximization for the firms, but it may be explicable in terms of income maximization for the promoters and financiers.[19] That is more likely in most cases than the rationalization and justification given by the raiders, namely that they will make the firms more efficient and in particular stop management from ripping off stockholders. Since they load firms with debt, it is not obvious that profit is the main motive. Maybe it is power the big raiders seek. Maybe it is the fun of a high-stakes game. Some of them take such big gambles that they lose rather than win, but the danger of losing does not seem to deter them.

If the *Business Week* analysis stresses growth and market share, that may be too simple also, but may be more realistic than the economics textbook. It is, of course, possible to interpret *Business Week*'s reporting as so biased by the views of the reporters that it misrepresents the major real concerns of the business decision-makers, so it is possible to assert that the economics textbooks are not biased and are better representing reality in treating profit maximization as the only major real motivation in business decision-making, as well as the only rational one. But the reporters are not building models out of their imaginations, they are trying to report what they find. The aim is empiricism, not simplified models. Perhaps economics could try to visualize the reporter's reality and try to explain it, rather than merely explaining models. Or they might import a little more complex human psychology into the analysis. It might yield a more realistic understanding of the world.

But what about small business? Although many people are employed by big business, the independent entrepreneur with just a few employees is by no means to be neglected. Is there something more that needs to be said about either such small business, or indeed about firms intermediate between the very large and the very small? The struggle merely to survive can indeed dominate some firms of any size, so considerations other than profit may be squeezed out. And for some firms that seem to have a secure place for at least a time, the old term "satisfising" may be applicable.

Certainly one of the important considerations from the point of view of social progress is the extent to which motivations, incentives, and situations conduce to decisions that promote technological progress or the sorts of innovations that are socially beneficial. More attention should be paid to what is known or can be learned about this.

Maybe the big business raiders, and perhaps those making other business decisions, are like other human beings. They may act on the basis of such a complex and shifting set of motives that it would take a mind-reading psychologist to specify the relative strength of different motives in any single decision. The mixture of motives may be so complex that even the object of study may be unaware of all of them and hence might not be able to report accurately in interview studies. More study of motivation and incentive response by business decision-makers would at least help improve upon the notion in economics that profit maximization, however profit rate may be measured, is the single all-sufficient explanation of business firm behavior.

There is in any case the question of the time horizon involved in profit-maximizing decisions. It is well known that there is often a conflict between short-run profit maximization and long-run profit maximization. The terms "short run" and "long run" are vague in this context, so we should speak of shorter- and longer-run time horizons. What can be said about the motivations, the incentives, and the situations that make shorter-run or longer-run time horizons predominate? Even if no generalizations can be adequately supported, mere exploration of the matter yields a more realistic view of decision-making than if such complications are omitted in favor of simple-minded profit maximization.

Where a major concern in business decisions is the effect on the price of a firm's stock, that in itself shortens the time horizon in the firm's decisions. This raises a real issue if the length of the time horizon is shortened to the point where it produces economic results for the country that are judged to be unfortunate. It is already clear that the firm should be more interested for its own sake in its longer-run profitability than in the immediate impact of any decision on its immediate stock price.

18. Oligopoly, Stability, and Public Policy

After you learn what the textbooks tell you about oligopoly, they should pose for you the problem of public policy. It should be explained that the nature of interdependence among oligopoly firms may lead to an unstable market situation. So-called cutthroat competition is one possible temporary outcome. Since that sort of situation is seldom desired by the oligopolists, even though they may drift into it at times, an oligopolistic industry may develop alternative ways of making it less likely and of preventing it in some cases. The literature on industrial structure and on antitrust problems indicates the various devices that have been employed at times by various industries. Some of these may be developed to introduce or maintain stability in an oligopolistic market. But the same devices can generally be used to develop and exert semimonopoly power in the market. The devices may be in effect collusive, although they may not be overtly so, and so they may escape antitrust action against them. The fact of price leadership in an industry may, for example, be difficult to attack successfully even if it exploits consumers. The problem is how to frame public policy so that it permits legitimate efforts to introduce stability into the oligopoly market and yet protects the public against the use of oligopoly power at the expense of others, including the consumers. Consideration of that should make for a good class discussion, and whoever comes up with an adequate solution should not only go to the head of the class but should be appointed attorney general and asked to advise Congress on how to write appropriate regulatory legislation.

19. Expectations, Uncertainties, and Probabilities

The economic principle is applicable whenever the given objective is maximizing something with scarce means and there is full knowledge of the relations between means and ends. Most microeconomic analysis is carried on by postulating, as if they were known, the relevant marginal magnitudes, be they marginal utilities, marginal productivities, or marginal costs and marginal revenues. That sort of analysis has direct usefulness where the magnitudes are indeed known, or where one can make quite good and reliable estimates of them. What one may actually know, though sometimes one does not have really good data on even this, is what the relevant magnitudes have been for some similar activities in the past. The future is inherently unknowable, but it is the future results of present or future decisions that are the needed basis for maximizing decisions, not the results of past decisions in circumstances that may not turn out to be exactly identical.

One necessarily bases decisions on *expected* magnitudes of marginal gains and marginal costs that would result from various decisions. The past is, to be sure, the first and perhaps the best basis for forming one's expectations of future magnitudes. Expectations need to try to take into account anything that suggests the future might be somewhat different from the past. If the expectations turn out to be fulfilled in all respects, after applying the marginal principle correctly, one will succeed in maximizing whatever one was trying to maximize. But the unforeseen and the unforeseeable may result in failure to maximize, despite rational behavior, though one may not know what would have been better even in retrospect unless it is possible to get enough data after the fact (and unless the data would not have been altered by one's different decision).

Uncertainty with respect to the future may be decreased if a decision is simply another in a long line of similar decisions in a situation that can reasonably be expected to be similar to many in the past. Looking at the results of such decisions in such situations may show the relative frequencies of various results, and if there is reason to expect the future to be similar, one can attach various probabilities to each result, based on the past experience. One might then act as though the most probable result is what will happen, or try to take into account also the possibility, and degree of probability, that something else might happen. If one or more of the other things that might happen creates a loss instead of the hoped-for maximized gain, the known past frequencies of losses provide a basis for some form of insurance against the undesired outcomes, especially if the present decision is only one of numerous comparable decisions being made by different people in a given short time period.

Where there is not such a statistical basis for such insurance, decisions are made in the face of various amounts of uncertainty, and the outcomes may or may not come close to those sought. It is a commonplace that, although decision-makers have different degrees of aversion to taking risks in the face of uncertainty, generally some chance of greater gain is needed to induce people to take risks if they could avoid them.

Oligopoly theory introduces a decision situation in which the result of a given decision by a firm depends on the reactions by other firms. The theory may be applicable in other situations, including various personal actions to which other people may react in different ways that affect the obtainment of one's objectives. International relations clearly need to be envisaged in terms of the relative likelihoods of various foreign reactions to a government's actions. In all such applications of the analysis, it is important to avoid wishful thinking and have some objective basis on which to form expectations.

If one sets up in a simple matrix the expected outcomes from different reactions of rivals to alternative actions a firm might take, it seems simple to decide on an action by choosing the one that might give the best result if rivals reacted as one would wish. But it may be relatively unlikely that rivals will act in a way that gives the best result. In oligopoly theory it is customary to assign probabilities to the various reactions of rivals to each decision a firm is considering. Then clearly one has a decision problem not reducible to the simple economic principle. A firm might base a decision on what are assumed to be the most likely reactions by rivals for each alternative action under consideration. One can see the rationale behind other decision rules that might be used. For example, the firm may choose so as to be sure to avoid a possible catastrophic loss. Or, if the situation is highly repetitive, it may calculate the statistical "expected value" of each action and alternative reaction and choose the highest expected value.

Such analyses are generally fun, and to some extent more realistic than analyses that assume that the results are always sufficiently well known and uncomplicated to decide action by applying the simple marginal principle. But the decision matrix is still an academic game. The real difficulty is that one generally does not know enough to be really confident in assigning probabilities to the reactions of others, and does not know enough to be confident in one's estimate of the outcomes even if others' reactions to one's own actions were known. There may be different degrees of uncertainty about these two things in any situation, and in different situations, and for different types of decisions. Textbooks do not go out of their way to emphasize these degrees of uncertainty, though uncertainty is the name of the game of economic decision-making, and indeed infuses all of life's decisions.

So while expectations are governed by many things, it is really uncertainty that prevails over risk. That should at least be recognized in the textbooks.

20. Externalities and Efficiency

The economics textbooks now introduce the concepts of external benefits and external costs as sort of a minor postscript to microeconomic analysis. The indication is that where some costs are external to a producer, too many resources are allocated to it by the market for maximum efficiency, and where there are external benefits, more resources should be allocated. The suggestion may be made that taxes and subsidies might be used to internalize the costs and benefits and thus achieve greater allocative efficiency. A common illustration of external costs is pollution by a producer, and a common illustration of external benefits is education (so-called, but really schooling). Here the only quarrel with the usual treatment of externalities is the usual paucity of instances and the treatment of externalities as sort of an addendum to microeconomics rather than as a major qualification of the whole corpus of conclusions usually reached in the main body of microeconomic theory.

It is not uncommon for a distinction to be made between private costs and social costs. Externalities may be discussed as instances where marginal private cost or benefit do not coincide with marginal social cost or benefit, and where it is therefore desirable from the point of view of efficient resource allocation for society to try to make the private and social marginals coincide. This embodies the only socially defensible principle; not much of a case can be made for letting some person's or firm's private net accounting override the net accounting that embraces everyone else.

But what should go into a full social accounting? We might well take the cue from the subtitle of a book by E.F. Schumacher, *Small Is*

Beautiful, subtitled *Economics as if People Mattered.* If the well-being of people is what it ought to be about, microeconomic analysis would have to focus substantial attention directly upon working conditions and living conditions. There should be as much attention to what is now loosely called the quality of life as to the quantity of goods and services produced, which are indeed related to well-being but not to be equated with it. There needs to be more talk about both the utilities and disutilities produced (and about the disutilities not reduced) by the manner in which the economy operates, and which may not be registered or registered adequately in the market price system. Some of this is external not only to the producer firms but also to the textbook analysis of them.

For example, the quality of the work experience can vary a great deal without that registering in costs borne by the firm and hence in market price, but it may make a whale of a difference in the utilities and/or disutilities of the work experience, or in plain language in the satisfactions and well-being of the worker. Cost to the firm and social cost may diverge. It may or may not actually cost the firm more per unit of output in some cases to alter the production process and to somehow exhibit more respect for the worker's ideas and feelings.

Economics has traditionally treated work as disutility, and indeed much of it necessarily involves disutility, sometimes very severe disutility. But it is also true that life is very much better when the work to be done is such that, or is organized so that, the worker can indeed find much satisfaction (utility) in its proper performance. The total utility produced might be easier to achieve now by improvements in the work experience than by the production of more "adult toys." Moreover, it should be clear that improving the work experience does not always have a net cost to a firm, although when it does, it might still be a proper cost to bear. Employees are very seldom provided incentive by the profit motive to work harder or to improve the quality of the products they work on. The connection is too indirect and often there is no actual connection. The employer can hire the workers, but how hard they work or how well is not just a matter of their pay. They are apt to respond very favorably to any number of incentives that add to their initial motivation. Often the worker knows better than the boss or foreman how best to do the job assigned. How well he or she works may depend heavily on whether the worker's opinion on such matters is sought, respected, and allowed to influence the work process. Attention to machinery safeguards, to any possible flexibility for the worker, to mechanizing simple repetitive operations that machines could do, to innumerable things that improve the work environment may pay off handsomely for a business.

But in any social accounting, the more that humane considerations play a part in organizing and carrying on the production process, the more efficient that production process can be said to be; that is, the higher its productivity in human well-being is likely to be. Of course, we cannot put numbers on human well-being or satisfaction in simple fashion, as the market can on money outlays or money receipts. So we write and study economics as though it was only about the numbers that we can talk glibly about. We sometimes dismiss what even those numbers are supposed to be about, as if that was in a realm that could be ignored because of lack of other simple numbers to measure it.

Similarly with respect to living conditions, these are in substantial measure produced by the economy. The disutilities produced or not reduced by the way the economy works (with much help from government, especially local democratic government) are not, as they might well be, treated as a part of basic economic analysis. Even courses on such specialties as urban economics are likely to devote much attention to the theory of location of firms, which, of course, is not irrelevant, but then relegate consideration of what might better be the heart of the subject, the quality-of-living conditions produced and the social consequences thereof, to the sociologist.

Is the Japanese economy to be considered efficient because it can export competitively in present circumstances although the living conditions of its workers are extremely poor, even by their own standards? Was our economy more efficient by employing some labor in so-called sweatshop conditions than if, even at greater monetary cost, working conditions had been humane? There is something wrong with our measure of efficiency if we say the sweatshop was more efficient. What is being said here is that the microeconomic analysis of the efficiency of the economy that confines itself to market measures and criteria of efficiency is defective and can be seriously misleading. Our criterion of efficient allocation of resources should explore externalities more fully. We should deal with social versus private costs and benefits, with utilities and disutilities not registered in market prices, at the heart of the analysis, rather than as a mere postscript. External benefits and costs are widespread. They are the general case, not to be dealt with as a minor postscript to the main analysis. We need to focus on what we know or can try to learn about working conditions and living conditions created. It is important how the economic process and its consequences treat people. We need to study economics as if people were all that mattered, as Schumacher implied. The human well-being created in the process or ignored or worsened is the most important thing about it. The simpler matters and the more readily measurable results to which the discipline confines itself are important but are not all-important or as important. Economics, at every point in the analysis, should be primarily about all that matters to people in the economic processes. After all, about half of the waking lives of employees are spent working. And women homemakers, who are usually not directly paid a wage for their work, typically work still longer hours, but economics textbooks totally ignore any issues that should be raised in that connection. How do we start to do so?

21. Responsibility to Stockholders and Others

The stockholders in a corporation are, in law, the owners of the firm, so, according to one ideology, the only criterion applicable in judging the firm's behavior is how well the firm does by its stockholders. Even that is not a totally unambiguous criterion, for it may have to do only with how high the dividend rate is, or it may lead to consideration of the growth of book value of the stock, or to the price of the firm's stock in the stock market at some time relative to book value, or simply to appreciation of the stock in the stock market (a matter affected by many things, some external to the firm), or it may require consideration of stock dilution, or the implications of debt burden and leverage, and so on.

Incorporation of a business venture can be a great advantage for many a business, which is why it has become a dominant form of business organization. A major advantage is the limited liability of stockholders, a limitation that is of importance in raising capital by spreading ownership of the firm. Bankruptcy law is also important in providing firms a legal way to cancel some of their debts, at the expense of their creditors, and to have another set of opportunities to make a go of it. The corporation is a legal creation, and as such is one of the most important social-economic inventions.

But just as no individual person or group can be allowed unlimited freedom without regard to the social consequences of their actions if society is to be even semicivilized, so no business firm, incorporated or not, can legitimately claim that any restraint upon its activities is unwarranted interference with its freedom or the freedom of its owners. Indeed, the major defense of the corporation as a legal creation is that, by granting it certain powers and privileges, society is better served than if the corporate form of business organization had never been invented. Society necessarily judges corporations, like other institutions and even individuals, in terms of their social contributions, not in terms of how well they do for themselves, perhaps even at the expense of others in society. The very existence of corporations as a legally created and socially favored form of business organization can be justified only by social consequences, as can the degree to which they are free or regulated or permitted to continue to operate.

The implication of this is that corporations are inevitably and properly judged, by those other than their ever changing owners, in terms that go beyond how well they do for their stockholders. This does not imply that owners are not entitled, within the legal framework that both benefits them and limits them, to try to advance their own interests, however they may be legally conceived. Indeed there are a number of ways in which they are free to try to do so. One of the most obvious is that disgruntled stockholders can sell their stock. This loses any legal power to change the firm's policy in the way they may have desired, but in some circumstances it may be their quickest and most effective way to protect themselves against further loss and to express displeasure with the management of the firm.

It is also true that a great deal of buying or selling stock may often have nothing to do with direct concern over a firm's conduct, about which buyers and sellers of stock often know very little. It may merely represent a guess as to what will happen to the price of the stock in the near future, and that may be primarily a guess as to what much of the rest of those operating in the stock market at the time will guess that most of the rest of the people in the market at the time will soon do in buying or selling that stock. To the extent that it is a market made by people trying to outguess what most of the rest of them will do, it is not primarily an expression of how well a generally stable body of owners thinks a firm is doing for them. It remains true, however, that individual owners can protect their interests to some extent and express their displeasure with a firm by disposing of its stock. It is also true that if the corporation has done too badly by stockholders, an individual's attempt to sell stock may entail a capital loss, so the protection is not complete. However, the capital loss may be due not to firm misman- agement but to the fact that developments in the firm's market quite beyond its control, even a general economic recession or depression, had a negative impact on it, no matter how well it was managed. In a sense, acquiring ownership of a firm's stock is itself a free choice to gamble upon that not happening, as well as upon firm management.

The major way for owners to protect and advance their interest in a corporation is through their legal power to hire and fire the board of directors, and thereby the management, and to determine the policies of a corporation. As everyone should know now, at least since the early study of *The Modern Corporation* by Gardner and Means, own- ership and control are not identical. A small controlling interest in a corporation may in effect render the bulk of stockholders powerless, given the mechanical and other difficulties in effective majority rule and the even lesser power of other minorities to protect themselves in and through voting in stockholder meetings. In many cases, once top management is in the saddle, over time it may be able to secure ap- pointment of its own chosen board of directors and thereby constitute itself a self-perpetuating corporate oligarchy. The strongest case for some unfriendly corporate takeovers is that it can throw out such en- trenched management or force it to operate more in the interest of the stockholders. The rub may be that the stockholders by that time are primarily financial operators in it for a stock market gain, not old-line owners seeking different policies, better handling of their money, or deserving better treatment by the firm in some respect. It may be clear that top management is rewarding itself too royally, especially when the firm is not or may not be able to do well, but raiders may also profit excessively by loading a firm with debt, so they are hardly able to pose well as saviors of stockholders. Raiders may also strip a firm of its accumulated cash, which may not always be defensible either. And when Wall Street busily engages in efforts to sell American firms to foreigners, it is hardly trying to protect their American owners.

Then there are the firms that set themselves target rates of profit; they might be reasonable or unreasonable. And if one of them does not make the target rate of profit, even though it may still be a very profitable firm, it may restructure, firing employees en masse, perhaps closing plants, and trying another tack to get the target rate of profit without regard to anything else whatsoever.

Whatever may be said about the adequacy of corporation owners' recourse to protect and promote their interests, as they see them, the public necessarily rejects the ideology that corporations are to be judged only in terms of how well they do for their ever changing stockholders or their often overpaid top managers. And management certainly knows that the public has every reason to judge them in additional terms, even when they sound as though they would prefer to defend the older ideology that stockholders are their only proper concern and that they have no public responsibilities. They cannot avoid knowing that their powers and privileges, which the law confers upon the corporation, necessarily imply some limits on what they can justifiably do, and entail some responsibilities to serve the broader society in return for the powers and privileges granted. Nor is it simply up to a corporation to decide what public responsibility it might choose to acknowledge. It is not always made clear that this ideological issue is what underlies much public debate over so-called government interference with business and its freedom. The textbooks are not doing their proper job if ownership is treated simply as freedom and obligation to maximize profits, for there are other interests that necessarily enter public concern.

Or as the matter is often put now, there are the other stakeholders, besides stockholders, who have an important stake in how the business operates. What needs to be discussed is broadly applicable to all forms of business organization, not only the corporation. All this the textbooks need to explore more fully than they often do. Three widely used economics-principles textbooks do not even have the stakeholder term in the index.

The stakeholder concept is explicitly rejected by some business spokespersons, but it is embraced by others who proudly proclaim how well their business serves the community. The concept is that business management has important responsibilities to all stakeholders, not simply those who are at least temporarily stockholders. It is not hard to identify other stakeholders and what their interest is. What a firm can do or should be expected to do to protect or further those interests, and how to balance the interests against each other, is far from clear, and requires much careful analysis. It is also hard to show how, if at all, the different stakeholders can now protect and advance their interest in the behavior of a business, and still harder to formulate public policy that would secure the most defensible balance among the various interests. But all this should call for serious analysis and much public discussion.

The employees of a firm are obvious stakeholders. Their concern is not only their income from the firm but how well they are treated by management. Labor unionism has been one method of trying to improve the pay received by some employees in some firms, but it has done more to check serious arbitrary actions of management in some cases than to affect the real wage rate of labor in general, a matter that depends more on the general level of labor productivity. Leaving a firm that treats its labor badly and taking jobs with other firms that treat it well has not, while formally an option, been as viable a real alternative as some ideologues would have us believe. As this is written, there appears to be increasing recognition that the respect given the opinion of the person doing a certain job, and improvement in the general treatment of the work force in a firm, can pay well in terms of increased labor productivity. True or not, it would be argued by some that any satisfaction in work performance possible in a production operation should be protected and promoted by one means or another for its own sake. It just might be that the nation's total utility or satisfaction could be directly increased more along this line than by any possible resulting increase in productivity of gadgets and adult toys for the big middle class that buys the bulk of the economy's output. These essays have already given attention to this and related matters, but it would be difficult to stress all such considerations too strongly if one is to learn properly what is really important in economics. The question that should be raised at this point is how best to promote employee interests and meet employee needs if that does not now occur "naturally" on a sufficient scale. Employees are a business firm's most important stakeholders and ones it daily affects directly over and over.

The customers of a firm constitute another stakeholder group that sometimes can protect itself by buying elsewhere if a market is sufficiently competitive, but in many cases they may not have a viable option or may not know enough how to protect themselves. For some products today, only a well-financed research lab testing a group of competing products could tell whether, if at all, the product really served the consumer interest as well as possible for the costs incurred. The textbook may speak highly of the market allocation of resources being determined by consumer sovereignty. But Nader's Raiders, while sometimes making statements that are too wild, can easily document cases where the consumer interest is not sufficiently considered by firms and could indeed be better served at similar cost. The issue for a business firm is sometimes short-run profit or long-run steady customers and long-run profitability. Good service to the consumer is now a proclaimed objective of many businesses, but whether this is advertising or the real objective is not always clear. At least there is a gain for consumers in that the "caveat emptor" slogan is heard less now and probably needed less now, though there are always enough scams around that the consumer still needs to be wary at times. The public policy question is, what is an optimal role for government in consumer protection? An attempt at complete protection would probably be regarded correctly as a cure that could be worse than the disease. But even one Thalidomide case, to take an example, is sufficient for most people to reject a completely laissez-faire approach. Consumers also want meat inspection and want autos to be free of defects that could cause fatal accidents. There are other examples of cases where consumers clearly want protection they cannot get just by market competition.

Consumer Reports is a private effort to research products in the interest of consumers, and its efforts are valuable, but its resources are too limited to keep up with continuous changes in products. Consumer sovereignty is said by the textbooks to be very important, and they assume it to be a reality. But they do not give much attention to the extent to which real consumer problems prevent any fully effective consumer sovereignty. The nature of advertising has already been mentioned in another essay, but needs consideration here as well. Textbooks do not give the same attention to the issue of an optimal public policy to ensure consumer sovereignty as they do to some other things, though the consumer policy problem is much more complicated. Fortunately the invisible hand about which we already spoke does reward business better for providing what consumers want than by producing things they do not want. And often competition takes the form of trying to serve consumers better. However, it is still true that business could often do much better by consumers as an important group of stakeholders than they do now. If they did, less regulation in the consumer interest would be called for or needed.

The suppliers of inputs to a firm should also be considered to be stakeholders of a sort. This is especially true when a single firm takes such a large portion of the supplier's potential output that its life or death depends upon the continuous renewal of a single order, and the supplier is under duress to accept the terms dictated by the firm it has become so dependent upon. One may counsel a firm never to become that dependent, but the question also is how any power over a supplier should be handled. Power is always something that can be abused. Responsible use of it avoids abusive use.

The general community in which any of a firm's operations is located constitutes a stakeholder also, and a very important one. Different firms' attitudes toward that stakeholder vary widely, which is often seen when a locally owned firm in a community is taken over by an absentee owner. Students may be aware of the problems sometimes arising with absentee ownership if their rooming house is not shared by the owner. Unfortunate is the community whose business firms have no concern for the community but only for top management and/or other stockholders. Firms typically make many decisions that affect the community favorably or unfavorably. To be sure, it is not easy to define how far that responsibility to the community should go, beyond avoiding harm. Many a town or city is a much better place to live, and indeed to do business in, if the business leaders use their clout and some of their firms' resources to improve the community itself. On the other hand, it can be very hard on a community to have a large firm suddenly close and move to another locality, though that sometimes happens. That harms more than its own employees.

Competitors are also a stakeholder, in a sense. Predatory pricing to force them out of the business is not unknown, nor are other forms of unfair competition.

It is sometimes pointed out that one stakeholder is unrepresented in the above list, the environment. The current health and long-run viability of the economy's natural resource base, its natural capital, is constituted by its entire natural environment. It is affected by pollution and depletion, the former usually dealt with in the textbook section on external costs and the latter often ignored in economics textbooks. The environmental movement may soon have more impact on economics-principles textbooks, as there are now entire courses on environmental economics. As yet there are no economies operating on a long-run sustainable basis. Some places in the world economy are overloading their life support system, overcropping, overgrazing, overfishing, and overforesting. Few topics are more important than soil conservation, but most principles textbooks do not have even a single chapter on agricultural economics. The only agricultural economics in most books stops with showing that price supports for agricultural products causes problems. Our fossil fuels give us much higher standards of living than was possible when the only energy we had was human energy or animal energy. They also cause pollution. In the long run the world will have to substitute various forms of solar energy for our economies. Is it too soon to invest in more research on how to do that? How much can business be expected to do to honor this stakeholder, and how much needs to be done by taxpayers and governments? Does the textbook help you wrestle with this? If not, do it on your own. There is now a lot written about the problems. We know, for instance, that business is sometimes given permission to clear-cut tracts in national forests and taxes are used to help pay to put in roads for the logging trucks.

Kenneth Goodpaster of the University of St. Thomas has wrestled with the question of just how a firm can handle its responsibilities to these stakeholders in the light of its fiduciary and legal responsibilities to stockholders. What responsibilities can firms bear, and what should government bear? This is an issue that deserves much more attention. Most economics textbooks ignore the stakeholder issues, but there is now a whole business-school textbook devoted to them: the third edition (1996) of Archie B. Carroll's *Business and Society,* subtitled *Ethics and Stakeholder Management.*

And in 1992 an organization of businesses was established to help firms that are interested in doing better by all their stakeholders. It is called Business for Social Responsibility and now has more than 1,400 members. That sounds good as a start, but it is a bare start.

No business needs to earn its profits in ways that are socially harmful. They should be allowed to operate only when they are operating in the public interest. Licenses and corporate charters ought to be revoked if firms refuse to clean up any of their acts that violate that principle. Short of that remedy, it may sometimes be possible to tax activities that are socially harmful. It should not be necessary to subsidize firms—that is, bribe them—to act in socially beneficial ways. The U.S. Supreme Court once ruled that a corporation has the same rights as an individual person under the law.[20] That ruling has had very unfortunate consequences and needs to be rejected now that it is perfectly clear that there is no resemblance between a person and what a person can do and a large corporation with its complex structure and all that it can do. Even the political clout of many big corporations needs to be curtailed, since it is clearly used to promote special interests instead of the general interest. If every union member must give written consent to a union political contribution, as some would have it, then every stockholder and every employee should have to give written consent (not just through a stockholder meeting) for a corporate political contribution. And corporate ownership of communications media should be limited to one per company. Those two changes would themselves do more to really democratize this country than many others could. It is somewhat unfortunate that economics now excludes any considerations that used to be included when it was called political economy. Clearly we need to study political economy.

The Distribution of Income and Wealth

22. Functional Income Distribution Theory

Non-Marxist economists no longer talk about the distribution of income among social classes but about the functional distribution of income, the return per unit to each of the economic factors of production that performs a function in the productive process. A single theory, the marginal productivity theory, in value terms, covers all. Every productive input will be paid according to its marginal value product. The question to be raised here is with respect to a "proof" of the marginal productivity distribution theory itself.

The proof usually offered is that firms could not afford to, or it would not be sensible to, pay more than the marginal value product of an input, and they could not get away with paying less due to competition for the input. It is assumed that both the firm and the input know the relevant marginal value product, that both are income maximizers, and that all input and product markets are perfectly competitive. It is implied that in any given case they both have viable and comparable alternatives.

But this does not show that the rates of pay are determined by marginal productivities of inputs, however identical the rates of return and the marginal value products may be, and however unprofitable it would be for firms to pay something different than marginal value products. In fact, the rates of pay could be determined by anything conceivable and the equation of marginal value product and pay could still hold. Pay could be determined by custom, by market power, by law, by flipping coins or by whatever method. The rates of pay having been set, profit-maximizing firms would then hire inputs up to the point—given diminishing returns, which is properly assumed—where their marginal value productivities would equal those variously determined rates of pay. Observed equalities between pay rates and marginal value productivities explain nothing whatsoever about what combinations of forces and institutions actually determine the rates of pay of different inputs.

The functional distribution of income requires an empirical analysis of institutional and other factors that may be operative in different factor markets. All that marginal value productivity can explain in any case is the quantities hired by the individual firm, given the pay rates somehow determined. One cannot escape this conclusion and reestablish the marginal value productivity theory of functional income determination by moving it to the macroeconomic level and aggregate demand curve, as will be shown later.

Anyone should be suspicious of the theory that marginal productivity determines wages and salaries from the simple observation of increases in such pay rates that have nothing to do with new marginal productivities of those receiving the pay. Other things explain the raises. And though product prices may be influenced, real pay rates are changed.

The labor markets determine over 80 percent of income, so their peculiarities are especially important, and they are not just like product markets, so they should receive special attention.[21]

23. The Minimum Wage Law

Although minimum wage laws are common, the economics textbooks seldom have a good word for them. More commonly the charge is made that while the intent of such legislation may be to improve the lot of part of the labor force, the effect is to harm some of those the laws are intended to help. The argument is that, given diminishing returns to labor, which cannot be disputed, and marginal productivity and pay necessarily equated, a minimum wage set by law above a market clearing level, or any increase in any such legal minimum wage, will necessarily result in a reduction in the number of laborers hired. Instead of having jobs at wages below what the law would designate, some labor will be without jobs at all. The conclusion is that minimum wage legislation is a bad thing, hurting some of those it is intended to help.

And that is all that is said about the matter. The issue is closed. Economics has condemned the minimum wage laws, though they remain, presumably because legislators and their constituents pay little attention to economic wisdom. Recently there have been attempts to ascertain whether the additional unemployment was of significant magnitude.

If someone says there is in any case still an ethical issue, that is not for economists to discuss; their policy conclusion is presumably devoid of ethical assumptions, and in any case ethics cannot invalidate economic conclusions. But perhaps there is room for the ethicist to pass the ball back into the economist's court on the basis of the ethicist's conclusions and see how much wisdom the economist can then muster.

An ethicist might contend that there is something seriously wrong with a relatively wealthy economy that can employ all its labor force only by paying some of them less than a "living wage" or in any case less than what others would generally find acceptable as a decent wage. The fact of the matter is that what is generally considered to be poverty in this country includes many people who are working "full-time" (about forty hours a week for fifty weeks) at low rates of pay. The so-called working poor are being exploited by those of us with middle-class incomes, whether the exploitation is intentional or not, because we are able to buy products of this labor in the market without paying a price that would cover decent rates of pay for the labor that produced the products. The bargaining power of the working poor is such that they cannot command a decent wage, so they take what they can get, and others benefit by indirectly employing them to make products at prices that don't cover what ought to be their costs of production if labor were decently paid.

The economist may be right that, other things remaining the same, raising a minimum wage level to relatively speaking "decent" levels would reduce employment and leave some of the working poor without any jobs at all, although the rest of the previously working poor might be raised above the poverty level by receiving a decent wage. That phrase, "other things remaining the same," leaves out the possibility that, in some periods, the rate of economic growth may be sufficient to permit a raising of the minimum wage without reducing employment of the labor affected. But let us consider the case where that is not possible, and some unemployment among the previous working poor is the price of raising the majority of the working poor out of poverty.

The question must then be faced squarely, is it not possible for the economy to employ these newly unemployed people at a decent wage, or is the only choice between their unemployment or large numbers of working poor? There would seem to be many things that would serve the community in one way or another, the value of which should cover their production at a cost that includes a decent wage for those producing the benefits. Economists know that there are many such things that do not get produced automatically in the market. The textbooks include discussion of some of these things under the category of "public goods," sometimes designated as an instance of market failure. But somehow it is not conceived as a market failure if all of the working poor must either remain so or some must be left unemployed because the market does not automatically find something they can produce that it will reward with a decent wage. One may wonder whether it is economic wisdom, or lack of sufficient real concern, or lack of imagination that induces economics textbook writers to leave the working-poor problem solved to their satisfaction by rejecting the minimum wage. They do so without a full exploration of whether we might generate some other alternatives for public consideration, alternatives that might do more credit to us and to the economy whose virtues the profession implicitly and often explicitly defends so strongly.

Employment may not even fall with a wage increase. A wage increase may lead the producers to increase the price of the product since their costs have risen. So the marginal value product of the labor also rises. John L. Lewis was regarded by my dad as the devil incarnate because he was going to bankrupt the coal companies with his wage demands. John L. Lewis forced the soft coal mines to pay higher wages to the miners, the price of coal went up, the marginal value product of the miners thereby went up, and the old equality between the wage rate and the marginal value product of labor still held. The coal companies did not really suffer and suddenly they paid a better wage to coal miners.

Perhaps everybody should have to pay prices that cover decent minimum wages, and a way should be found to create enough jobs if some are left out as a consequence. That is the intent of those who support minimum wage legislation. The real problem with minimum wage laws is something else instead. In practice minimum wage laws sometimes boost the whole wage structure, because "customary" wage differentials are restored in the collective bargaining process or otherwise.

It is apparent that this part of the problem can be solved only by compression of the wage structure. The minimum wage might need to be set in reference to some median or other benchmark wage rate. It would be necessary to do this so it cannot lead to a continuing wage spiral in which the relative minimum wage set by the law never catches up or stays caught up. Wage inflation could become continuous if higher-wage recipients were allowed to keep trying to maintain the old differentials over the minimum wage every time it was increased to compress the wage scale.

It should not be necessary for the federal government to pay a supplementary wage to those being paid poverty-level wages. That would amount to a subsidy to their employers, and one can readily imagine how over time the number of such employers, delighted to get labor at substandard wages, would grow to take advantage of such a subsidy. But government might raise the disposable income of poverty-wage recipients by relieving them of state and federal income taxes, social security taxes, and Medicare contributions. The earned income tax credit does help.

24. Marginal Productivity as an Implicit Ethical Norm

Although positive economics explicitly rejects the notion that it embodies any ethical judgments, it seems implicitly to support the notion that pay according to marginal value productivity is the proper basis for income distribution in any economy, as well as explicitly arguing that it is the necessary basis in a market economy. We have argued that the actual distribution in a market economy could be affected by many different things, so that marginal productivity may not be the determining one. But many people would likely accept without argument that it ought to be determining. Marx espoused the idea that a man is entitled to the fruit of his own labor, but Marx had no monopoly on the idea that people should be paid according to their worth, which is to say according to the value of their contribution to society. And their contribution to society is often measured by their contribution to the productive process. Or, if there is a difference, at least an employer can be expected to pay only the contribution to the employer's productive operation. It is common knowledge through history that the contributions of some individuals to human well-being have vastly exceeded their contributions to their employer. One thinks of inventors, developers of vaccines, and so on. There is no way for later generations to reward them according to social contribution. And there may be only limited ways for their own generation to reward them monetarily in relation to their value even to their own generation. But laying aside these considerations, there is still the notion that most labor ought to be paid according to its contribution to the value of the products it helps produce for the market.

A basic difficulty with the concept, however, is that labor's productivity depends upon so much besides the individual laborer. The theory of eventually diminishing marginal productivity, as it is properly called, makes explicit that the marginal productivity of any factor of production depends heavily upon the quantities of other factors of production used with it in a joint production process. Either a cross section or a historical analysis makes it clear that the productivity of labor is very highly dependent upon the capital-to-labor ratio. Labor productivity, especially in some sectors of the economy, has been increased tremendously by the increased amount of productive capital equipment per laborer. That makes it possible for a firm with a capital-intensive productive process to pay higher wage rates than a firm can with a labor-intensive process, other things being equal. But the implication of this is that it is not just the labor that is to be credited for high productivity of labor or given the blame for its low productivity. That touches the idea of merit, of course.

Probably no one would dispute the idea that someone who loafs on the job deserves less pay than the person who works conscientiously. Even the more extreme forms of egalitarianism seldom would deny that. A problem that many people have with schemes in this country or in other countries that make a worker's income depend upon the productivity of the group of which the worker is a part is that the income is then affected by what others do or do not do, and not solely upon one's own effort and success. And it would seem that a direct incentive of lower pay for a loafer would be more productive for society than reliance upon group pressure on its members to hold up their end of the job. It may be surprising then that this country's pay systems do not often vary pay with individual output. The pay is set for different types of work, and everyone fitting a certain category of labor or job is paid by the hour, or in other positions is paid a fixed salary, in neither case varying with individual output on that job. History explains why piece-rate systems of pay were often eliminated when labor unions developed power to eliminate them; namely, the system was abused by employers' lowering piece rates in order to speed up work when finding that labor could indeed speed up.

But let us consider piece-work pay that is geared to a worker's marginal value productivity. The simple fact is that in any work situation the worker's productivity depends not only on the individual's own skill and effort, but upon the activities of others over whom the individual does not have control. On an assembly line, the individual's pace is set, though sometimes the quality of the individual's work may vary, in that the job may not be properly done. In any firm, how well management does its job can affect substantially the quantity of work the individual subordinate employee can do in any given period. If, because of poor management, the flow of parts needed is not available, labor's productivity is adversely affected. Indeed factors external to the firm can affect the ability of labor to turn out the work it otherwise would. So it turns out that the objection to basing pay on group production is the same as that to systems nominally basing pay on individual output. Output is heavily dependent upon other people, including management.

It may seem a bit anomalous also that a person whose individual output is as good as ever should find their pay going up and down with every change in the market demand for the product or service involved. That, of course, is entailed in pay by marginal value product. Seasonal, cyclical, or secular economic changes value a product or service differently over time. Long-run changes of this sort are expected to properly stimulate some movement of labor and other resources toward or out of individual lines of production. The problem is that the market valuation of a product at any time depends in part upon the distribution of income itself. Justification of that distribution must therefore precede a justification for paying a laborer according to the market's valuation of the laborer's output.

Presumably everyone would argue for varying pay according to effort insofar as it is possible to do so, since loafing and conscientious work have quite different merit. The above considerations show that things beyond the control of the individual typically affect the output of the worker or affect its value, and pay according to effort alone is not possible or desirable.

But often people talk as though pay according to ability is right. Indeed the present distribution of income and wealth is often explained as just a reflection of people's relative ability. Paying according to ability to perform the work of a firm would have some of the same practical difficulties for a firm that we have already discussed. But we are talking now about norms. Would there be a case for trying to improve the distributive system so it would reward people according to ability? Talk about pay according to ability seems to assume that ability can be ranked on a single scale to start with, and that we can indeed measure people on that scale. But clearly we must talk about ability in the plural, even though some people rate higher with respect to some combination of abilities than do other people. When we shift to talking about various abilities, there is the obvious fact that people rate relatively high with respect to some ability or abilities and relatively low with respect to other abilities. The question becomes, what should be society's level of reward for different abilities? Ability to sing, to fiddle, to play a horn, to play a sport, to weld, to use a jackhammer, to saw, to plumb, to invent, to manage, to soldier, to teach at different levels is not the same for all people, so what does "reward according to ability" really mean? History and anthropology show that different societies, or any given society at different times, place different values on different abilities. Reward according to ability is so vague as to be practically meaningless until one specifies a scale of rewards differentiating among types of abilities as well as according to the degree possessed of each ability.

Then one needs to bring together the concepts of ability and effort in some fashion, since effort matters ethically. Not much of an argument can be made that any specified ability should be equally rewarded whether or not it is used to benefit society or is allowed to lie unused. A still more basic question is whether society should reward people according to inherited abilities or only according to what they have done to develop and apply those abilities. A skill that one has developed, based on inherited potential, seems more worthy of reward than the inheritance of potential.

Going beyond this it is an odd concept of justice that would say that people whom nature has already rewarded with great ability of some sort should be further rewarded by society all their life for having been born so lucky, while society should further penalize those whom nature deprived of special degrees of any specific ability. It might better be argued that society should expect more from those endowed well by nature and treat that endowment as its own reward, while offsetting to some degree nature's deprivation of other people. We do tend to accept some obligation to those deprived by nature, but the offset is usually not much more than what is needed to make life somewhat bearable.

It is not the intent of this brief discussion that economists need to become ethicists also, or that the principles of economics textbooks need to give a full and adequate treatment to the ethics of the distribution of income and wealth, but that at least some brief discussion is needed to make students aware that the usual textbook marginal productivity theory of distribution cannot properly be taken as automatic, sole, and sufficient justification for its being treated as normative. It does not suffice simply to say so in so many words, because it is likely to be taken as a norm unless at least a few of its difficulties are presented. And since distribution is so important to everybody, and such concepts as the ability concept tend to be tied to the marginal productivity concept, a word about such is also needed to stimulate students to think about parts of accepted ideology—not to provide a different normative answer, but to disabuse them of the notion that economics has given a definitive answer to a question that involves a variety of ethical issues.

25. More on the Distribution of Income and Wealth

The marginal productivity theory of distribution deals only with the functional distribution of income by purportedly explaining the pricing of productive services in the factor of production markets. That pricing, however done and explained, is only the first step in determining the income of any person, household, or family. The textbooks usually say that that income, the personal or size distribution of income, is determined by the pricing of productive services and the distribution of ownership of such productive services. And so it is. But there is no textbook explanation of the distribution of ownership of productive services, as important as that is. The reason for the omission is that there is no economic theory to explain it. Only history explains it, that is, describes its evolution. Clearly it is partly a result of the operation of an economy over time, the results cumulating. As popular ideas have it, not incorrectly, it takes money to make money, so to some extent inequality tends to grow. "Shirtsleeves to shirtsleeves in three generations," another popular saying, indicates that excess stupidity can crop up in any family line at times. It can happen, but even moderate prudence would enable the wealthy to become wealthier if their gambles were confined to half their wealth while the rest was invested safely at compound interest. Clearly in an economy of rapid and to some extent unforeseeable change, riches to rags, rags to riches, and other changes in the distribution of income and wealth can come about through the impact of change on the distribution of ownership of productive resources.

Obviously the distribution of ownership of productive resources is affected also by the tax structure, especially as it deals with the passing on of wealth from one generation to the next. Custom and tradition also affect that historically. In a culture where the farm or business is passed on to the eldest son, the outcome over time is very different from that in a society where family assets at death are divided among the children in some other way.

The degree of inequality in the distribution of income is due more to inequality in the distribution of ownership of income-producing wealth than it is to inequalities in the pricing of people's productive services, large though the latter is in some cases. There are obvious examples of huge incomes of sports stars, entertainment stars, business executives, and financiers because of the prices they can charge for their personal services. But inheriting or acquiring a lot of income-producing assets enables one to quite outdistance in the economic race most of those who must rely solely on what their own productive services can yield. Henry George pointed out the unearned capital gains conferred upon owners of urban land as a result of population growth. In addition to the fact that interest can be compounded safely on some capital, that which is placed at risk tends in the aggregate to earn a higher return even net of losses. For most people, earnings on personal services can't begin to keep up, let alone catch up, to income earned by initial property ownership, even by saving to acquire property.

The elites are now the wealthy, and like all elites throughout history, they claim entitlement to their position by virtue of some alleged superiority, always a convenient rationalization, but also generally a spurious one. When one hears credit given to or taken by businessmen for creating the wealth of the country, not just their own wealth, one can give due credit to their important role. But the GNP is indeed a joint product, not produced by the business leaders alone, nor are they the only vital factor, as they could produce none of it alone. A better perspective might be obtained by hearing at the same time the sort of thing I once heard from a laboring man who was protesting loudly and bitterly that he and others like him had been the ones who had sweated and burned themselves out physically in building the roads, the railroads, the bridges, the products about which the bosses bragged, while the bosses had sat in their plush offices shuffling papers. How should the credit be distributed?

What gets distributed unequally is not only the praise but the output itself. That is what was referred to at the outset as the "for whom" question—for whom is the output produced. Clearly it is produced for people in accordance with the incomes they spend, for consumer goods and services, and for capital goods to earn some of them more income. The allocation of resources is determined by the combined spending patterns of households, businesses, and governments.

The high degree of inequality of household income accounts for the fact that, as the critic says, the economy efficiently serves the rich. More specifically, it is an efficient use of resources to build luxury apartments and offices for the rich than to build housing for the poor or to meet even their basic needs. When we talk about the efficiency of our economy, this is one of the things it means in practice, given the high degree of inequality of wealth and income that economics is often taken to defend. It should at least be easy to understand the outlook of the critic. But is there not more that economics can say about income inequality? Yes, it says that inequality of income serves to perform several important economic functions. Let us examine these briefly, or reexamine them even if the basic textbook does.

Especially for less developed countries, there is controversy over whether economic development requires a high degree of inequality, whether a high enough degree of inequality produces development or instead hinders it, and furthermore whether development necessarily increases the degree of inequality in a country.

Since most saving comes from the upper-income groups, and since saving is important to finance the sort of investment in capital equipment and technological progress upon which higher future productivity depends, substantial inequality of income is essential to promote such progress. Historically the case is solid. Yet socialist critics sometimes contend that it is outrageous for a country to depend for its real investment rate upon the fraction of their excessive incomes that the wealthy decide not to use for high living or for investment in other countries, and they say no country need do so. The critics are right also. Any country could decide upon what fraction of its resources to devote to domestic real investment and research and development and tax itself to finance it insofar as voluntary saving does not. For any given amount of such investment, the reduction in the general public's consumption can be the same whether caused by taxation or by the diversion of resources to feed the consumption of the rich. So inequality does serve to promote real investment, at a rate determined by private judgments of the rich themselves, though the rate could be determined politically, whether democratically or in an authoritarian framework. If government did supplement whatever saving the rich invested in their country, the tax funds destined to increase the rate of investment need not be invested directly by government. They could be lent to private enterprise at some appropriate rate of interest and proper security. But government need not rely entirely on where private enterprise might choose to invest the funds; government would have the added advantage of being able to determine where the investment would be most important from the point of view of the country's development. It might be in improving infrastructure instead of, for example, movie theaters.

Now back to another function of inequality. In the face of changes in tastes, resources, and technology, it is necessary for an economy to reallocate resources to maintain an efficient allocation. Inequality can serve to promote such reallocation if returns to resources decline in sectors that need to contract and increase in other sectors, and in fact such changes in returns do occur and do serve to promote reallocation and hence efficiency. It should be pointed out, however, that even if such changes in rates of return did not occur, the change in opportunities for employment of resources in different lines of production would serve to promote the needed resource reallocation.

The other major economic function served by inequality is said to be incentive to higher productivity by each factor of production. Insofar as effort to achieve higher productivity is directly rewarded by higher rates of return, inequality clearly serves to help perform that very important function. We have already pointed out the lack of correspondence between pay for individual laborers and their effort, despite universal sentiment that effort deserves reward compared to laziness.

There is another lack of correspondence, that is, between income and need. Not everyone's needs are the same, but ethically there should be a close relation between need and the income available to meet it. If the relationship were closer, that would strike people as more fair, and as such itself have an incentive effect.

But what needs some rethinking is the ideology that supposes that it is the profit motive that is the sufficient and all-important economic incentive to higher productivity in our economy. Carrot and stick, profit and loss, with the real emphasis on the importance of there being adequate profit in all business endeavors, can and do help provide incentive for a high degree of effort by entrepreneurs and top management and affect their contribution to productivity. However, it requires very little objective thought to recognize that for most economic effort, for most economic decisions by most people involved in production, there is no direct profit recompense for trying harder. Of course, everyone contributing to a business is affected by whether the firm makes enough profit to continue to employ them. Profit depends upon many things besides the amount of any one individual's effort. They may get higher income from it if it makes more profit. But the market may dictate less profit even from greater effort. So it is easy to exaggerate the directness or even the indirect importance of the profit motive. In the absence of a direct profit-sharing plan, the profit incentive is often very indirect and may be less important in incentive than other things. In the corporation, stockholders get the portion of the profits that top management decides to provide, the rest being added to reserves or spent by the firm. Greater or lesser profits to stockholders can hardly be claimed to motivate their efforts to increase firm productivity, about which they typically have nothing to say, although it may lead them to sell their stock, perhaps making it more difficult for management to attract capital to improve the firm's productivity. As for management, we have expressed skepticism as to whether the profit incentive really dominates them.

The ideology justifying much inequality relates to the share needed by the risk taker, those whose wealth is at risk when invested in plant and equipment or in development and marketing of new products, and so on. Indeed classical economics justified interest partly on the ground that the lender of capital was sacrificing present consumption, and interest was a reward for the sacrifice. It is a little strained to use the term "sacrifice" when some people are in a position to grab such a large portion of current income that it would be hard to spend it, so they invest it and make more income later. Prudent people don't risk much that they cannot afford to lose, though there are gamblers, of course, who can be enticed to invest by even small chances of big winnings. Milking gamblers is now a way of raising money, so they don't need a net return in the aggregate. But in general it can be admitted that the kind of economic risk taking that produces innovations, for example, requires not only a chance to lose but a net chance to gain, that is, a net return for risk bearing. But the aspect of rewards for risk bearing that goes unnoticed by economists is that the capitalist typically risks what he can afford to lose, while the labor employed in the risky enterprise gets no extra wage for risk but, if the venture fails, loses a whole livelihood. Labor risks more than just extra capital, and may often have more difficulty getting other jobs than the capitalist has in recouping his capital in another venture. What is an equitable return to what kind of risk, and why is it easier to get reimbursed for one kind of risk than for a more devastating one? In any case, what the capitalist risks is typically not his own but someone else's money. The someone else may not get rewarded as well as the capitalist when the investment pays off, but may take a bigger share of the risk of complete failure.

But granted that inequality serves to some degree to perform the important functions just discussed, the question becomes how much inequality can be justified on each of those grounds, since each function can be performed to some degree without it. Might we not expect diminishing returns to inequality also? The tendency in some quarters seems to be to rationalize whatever degree of inequality happens to exist at any time, but surely there must be some limit to the degree of inequality that can be justified by its economic functions. The higher the degree of inequality, how strong can the justification be? How much does deservingness, on any grounds, differ among people? How much distortion in the allocation of resources is justifiable to help perform each economic function to which inequality can contribute? How much should the rest of the public be expected to contribute in real resources to higher living by the rich in order to provide them enough income to induce them to invest another million dollars in what they decide is the most rewarding real investment? John Rawls, in a noted work, *Theory of Justice,* appears to accept as justifiable any increase in the wealth of a few if it results in any improvement in the lot of the poorest. Is any ratio of gain at the top to gain at the bottom OK, any increase in the degree of inequality so easily justified?

It has been charged that a large degree of inequality of wealth and income has some adverse effects on political democracy. The Marxist view that government is simply the instrument of a ruling wealthy class even in democracy is obviously refuted by the evidence of legislation contrary to that class interest. But anyone who cannot see the special political influence of such a class must have eyes that do not want to see.

Inequality thus raises questions that go beyond the poverty problem, which is more than a problem of the working poor. Extensive poverty is inexcusable in an economy as productive as ours. If economics were concerned with human beings, the causes of various types of poverty would be analyzed at length, along with detailed discussion of the merits and demerits of alternative ways of dealing with each type. At least that should not be too much to expect of principles of economics textbooks.

Then there is the further question of whether inequality can become so great that it creates a problem of maintaining full employment. Clearly an extreme can be imagined at which there would unquestionably be an employment problem. If 95 percent of income were obtained by the wealthy and 5 percent by everyone else, and if the wealthy desired to save and invest 90 percent of national income and consume only the other 5 percent, it seems evident that the 90 percent invested could not provide expected profits when only 10 percent was consumed. Or if it did, it could not continue to generate further inequality and full employment indefinitely. It requires high levels of purchasing to yield adequate positive returns to investment, and so to maintain the rate of investment.

In any case, Keynes was not wrong that any constant level of employment requires that saving (indeed all leakages) be offset by real investment (or total injections into the income stream). Continuous full employment is not ensured when savings are not used for real investment but are used to buy up other firms, downsize them, and reward Wall Street and the raiders handsomely. We may not have a shortage of saving when this is how it is used. But there are limits to how high the saving rate can go and still be effectively used to create jobs.

Schumpeter was right that real innovation increases the potential for real investment. But is there no limit to the amount of inequality and saving that innovative real investment can always offset? The higher the savings ratio, the bigger the burden on innovation to make up for it even while consumption is low. Schumpeter may have been too pessimistic about the conditions necessary for high rates of innovation, though he was undoubtedly right that each innovation produces a period of market growth, followed by a period in which there is only replacement demand for any new product. Then new innovation is required. Sometimes it occurs when needed, but it cannot be expected to do so without limit if inequality and saving grows without limit. The so-called optimum propensity to consume depends partly on the rate of innovation, but there is certainly a bigger problem to maintain full employment continuously when inequality becomes very great. The greater the inequality, the higher the needed rate of continuous innovation. It may not always be forthcoming at the needed rate. Then recession or depression unemployment develops until something pulls a country out of it. Prosperity is not likely to be maintained indefinitely with too high a degree of inequality.

26. The Equity–Efficiency Trade-off

In 1975, the Brookings Institution published a little book by Arthur Okun entitled *Equality and Efficiency: The Big Tradeoff,* which will likely come to be considered a classic in its field. I highly recommend the book, not because I take exactly the same position on all the issues as does Okun, but because it is as good a book as I know to help people think about some of the issues. Okun is a reasoning and reasonable person. The book is not spent shooting down the straw man of complete equality. Okun is instead talking about the potential trade-off between efficiency, as measured largely by the market, and lesser degrees of inequality than markets tend to produce. If I understood him correctly, he does see an equity problem, but in the end he thinks we should not worry too much about trying to get as complete a solution to that problem as some others would advocate.

Our discussion of the distribution of income and wealth is concluded here with a little further elaboration and summary of the relations among equity, equality, and efficiency. Textbooks often indicate that policy issues involve equity considerations that lie outside the realm that economics can say anything about. But they may suggest that equity considerations might be expected to conflict with efficiency considerations. One might get the impression that equity means equality, and that is enough for many people to reject the matter out of hand. Besides, efficiency is obviously desirable, so why sacrifice it for some dubious conception of equity? There are indeed potential conflicts between equity and efficiency considerations at times, and one should therefore investigate the trade-off ratios specific to different instances of conflict. But the argument here will be that if we give serious attention to what we want efficiently to achieve or promote, it would lead to a revised notion of how to conceive of and measure efficiency, and much of the conflict with equity would disappear.

What egalitarians typically insist is not that equal incomes would be equitable, and they certainly never claimed that people are equal in any biological characteristic in which they clearly are not, but they do argue that people should be treated as having equal rights in some basic respects. They should have equal right before the law and an equal right to vote. They should receive equal justice, have an equal opportunity for education, an equal right to speak their minds, an equal opportunity to worship in whatever religion they hold, and so on. Egalitarians hold that all people, whatever their various differences, should also have equal economic opportunities. They usually also think that excessive degrees of inequality in social outcomes, such as now exist, are not equitable.

The discussion of income distribution in the preceding section is egalitarian in that sense. It does not indicate everything that would need to be considered in formulating one's conception of equity, but perhaps enough is said to show why complete equality of income and wealth is not implied. That is the case for most egalitarians, if for no other reason at least because one cannot defend as equitable giving the loafer as much income as the conscientious worker on any job whatsoever.

What gets repeated emphasis relates to the common notion, elaborated with much insight by Okun in the book cited, that there is a conflict between and hence a trade-off between equity on one hand and efficiency on the other. If these concepts are defined as usual, Okun's discussion should receive nothing but praise. But the suggestion being made here is that there is something wrong with an efficiency concept that finds an economy operating efficiently when it allocates resources to producing superfluous luxuries for a few while it leaves simple and important basic needs for others unmet. For the most part economists have tended in the past to take anything the market does as defining an efficient allocation of resources, and other economies are defined as inefficient insofar as resources are not allocated by a market. The only qualification made in one section of principles textbooks was with respect to monopoly, but that was not taken so seriously as to deny that the market was, with only a very minor exception, the definer of efficient allocation. There has been some improvement in recent years in recognition of other market failures to allocate efficiently. Economists no longer ignore the failure of the market to deal with externalities or public goods. Public goods are simply to be taken out of the market in general and provided by government. Market allocation of everything else is held to be only slightly distorted and slightly inefficient insofar as it fails to internalize the externalities. It has already been argued that externalities are generally involved. They are not the exception but the general case. But there is something more that needs attention. If mentioned at all, little attention is paid to the distortions caused by excessive stuffing of the market ballot box by the rich at one end of the income scale and the relative and absolute serious underrepresentation of the poor in voting in the market at the bottom end of the income scale.

If we pay any serious attention to the relative urgency of human wants, needs, well-being, or even satisfactions, surely it is an odd concept of efficiency that refuses to acknowledge that the contribution to meeting none of these can be maximized in a market in which great income inequality produces large market distortions in resource allocation. Surely the public does not consider the present allocation between rich and poor equitable, else there would be no public concern shown over the plight of the poor. It is not efficiency we would be giving up to some degree by allocating more resources to increasing the utilities or basic human satisfactions of the poor, and less to satiating some of the satisfactions of the rich. It would be achieving greater efficiency in any really sensible meaning of the term "efficiency." We should satisfy urgent needs before we satisfy superfluous wants. It would be meeting needs that should be valued more highly. It would be increasing the total value by a resource reallocation. It would be a more efficient use of resources.

In any human sense, the economy might be judged to be efficient only insofar as it produced what the public considered to be an equitable division of the economic pie. It would not be considered efficient to surfeit some people with luxury goods while the basic needs of others were unmet. Given such a conception of efficiency, there is no conflict and hence no unfortunate necessity of being subject to a trade-off between equity and efficiency. We are back to the concept of social value again, something not measured by the market when it is distorted by huge income inequalities as it is. An efficient economy is in this sense one that would allocate resources so as to maximize social value, not market value alone. So the market test of efficiency is simply wrong if this criterion is used.

It may be objected that I am introducing interpersonal utility comparisons, which economics says are not allowable. If so, I would insist that in real life situations, however difficult for scientific economic analysis, such comparisons need to be made when equity is at issue. Actually I did not use the term "utility," but dealt with the marginal value to the poor of having urgent needs met as against the marginal value to the rich of another luxury. That is sufficient for the argument.

The real trade-off is obviously between the interests of the rich and those of the poor. More of the pie for one means less of the pie for the other when we are speaking of the allocation of a given volume of resources between the two. To be sure, the ideology that rationalizes unlimited inequality claims that the more income at the top, the more trickles down to others, and that anything that reduces inequality hurts those it is intended to help. This self-serving argument has an element of truth to it, but only an element; it is not the whole truth and nothing but the truth. Indeed if taken too far it contains more than an element of falsehood. There is surely some limit to the number of luxury cars provided to the so-called rich tycoon that will be an efficient way of meeting the basic needs of the poor. In terms of even an unreconstructed efficiency concept, the most efficient way of meeting the needs of the poor is not increasing the incomes of the rich to get a part of it to trickle down to the poor. Furthermore, trickle-down does not always work. Clearly there is something wrong with an economy when wealth and poverty grow at the same time at the expense of the middle class.

Perhaps in terms of conventional efficiency, equity considerations are simply ruled out. Then people concerned with equity must simply insist that attention be paid to equity, and we are back to the question of what in given instances the trade-offs might be. How seriously would efficiency be harmed, how much would total market output be reduced to divide income somewhat more equitably so no one would be in poverty? Equity would require that much sacrifice in market efficiency. While I cannot prove it, I am sure the sacrifice would not be large, and that it would be fully justifiable.

What business entrepreneurs want, and what people high in the income scale want, if we judge by the noise made in economic policy debates, is unrestricted economic opportunities. They want to be able to do anything that they may take a notion to do to increase their economic privileges and power, of which they already have the lion's share. Those lower in the income scale would be unable to take advantage of such unrestricted freedom, for they have not the wealth to do so. Economic freedom does not have the same meaning for everybody.

What everyone lower in the income scale wants is primarily security in a good job and, secondarily but still important, some prospect of that job or some other attainable job paying somewhat better in the foreseeable future. At times there is a conflict in most of us between exercise of unrestricted freedom by the first group and the concerns of the second group. It is seldom clear exactly what the trade-off terms are, but the issue clearly involves equity as between the interests of the two groups when there is a conflict. As has been said already, the conflict is not absolute, since there is also a degree of mutual interest of both groups in the enlargement of the pie so both can have larger pieces. There may even be a trade-off between enlarging the pie more and sharing the pie better. But the well-off have no equity ground for refusing to deal with the equity of the sharing when the pie is enlarged, of which they are generally the major beneficiaries. It is not sufficient to base an argument on the ground that the pie might grow a little more if their share was never touched. And it is by no means clear that that is the issue. Excessive inequality may reduce rather than increase the size of the pie by producing unemployment. That is dealt with elsewhere.

Let us talk of the broader issue here, the issue of the way the gains and costs of economic change are shared. Equity is not only a matter of the relative shares in the gains of economic progress, but of how the costs of progress are shared. Economic insecurity is caused by economic change. The threat can materialize in at least temporary losses and hardship, and it sometimes throws people upon the economic scrap heap. The economic benefits of change to the nation may be considerable, but the costs may be imposed upon a few who may be unable to handle them very well if at all. The equity question is not whether the change should be permitted if it hurts somebody who can't handle it.

The question is whether there is a way for the cost to be shared by those who reap the benefits. Equity would not be served by denying the majority in the nation the potential benefits in order to avoid an inequitable burden upon a few. Nor would it be served by ignoring an obviously inequitable distribution of the costs of change. It is safe to say that the economy would become increasingly inefficient if resource allocation did not respond to changes in tastes, resources, and technology, and that no case in equity can be made for blocking all change, though equity does require attention to the sharing of costs as well as benefits. The costs must not be imposed predominantly upon labor. Labor must not simply be dumped on the scrap heap of change and progress.

It is possible to formulate an equitable socioeconomic policy objective that embraces what everyone is entitled to and in fact does demand as a right, and which at the same time produces what compatibility there can be between the concerns of the two groups discussed above, concerns for freedom, security, and economic improvement. The objective of policy would be to provide, insofar as possible, fair and ample opportunities for everyone to develop their fine potentialities. The word "fair" has to be defined in terms of whatever is the public consensus. For a society to operate democratically, it is necessary that there be at least some consensus in that respect. Everyone knows how they do and don't want to be treated by others, and that provides a minimum content for the terms "fair" and "fine." Any culture has at least some degree of consensus as to those concepts.

Important as fair and ample opportunities are, there are limits to how far they can be equalized, and limits to how far the power to utilize opportunities can be equalized. Given that fact, the case for paying no attention to how unequal the outcomes may be is not very solid. Human needs are not equal either, and outcomes should take these inequalities into account. One can call it either more efficient or more equitable to do so. Equality of outcome cannot be defended, but neither can just any degree of inequality that results in an economy.

Macroeconomics

27. Aggregate Demand and Supply

Many textbooks begin their macroeconomic analysis by presenting. aggregate demand-and-supply curves that look very similar to short-run demand-and-supply curves for a perfectly competitive industry. Students may easily suppose that one can get the aggregate demand-and-supply curves simply by adding up such industry demand-and-supply curves. Before being given an alternative explanation, students should be told why simple aggregation does not work. The purpose of this essay is to show that there are problems with the concepts of aggregate demand and supply even as they are usually explained now. This will include a review of what it is legitimate to lock in caeteris paribus when drawing any demand-or-supply curve, and what we can legitimately treat as independent variables.

The first argument is that, since no economy is perfectly competitive even in the short run, the aggregate demand-and-supply curves cannot be obtained by summing "normal shaped" demand-and-supply curves appropriate only for perfectly competitive industries. Essay 11 explained why such "normal" demand-and-supply curves do not represent price and output determination correctly for the industries that actually dominate our economy. So even for that reason, simple aggregation is not possible.

Aggregate demand-and-supply curves should not in any case treat the price level as the independent variable to which quantities demanded and supplied at various price levels are represented by the curves. The price level cannot be taken to be a truly independent variable to any great extent. Textbooks still sometimes initially present the curves as though that were the case, however. Then they give an alternative explanation of the shapes of aggregate demand-and-supply curves. That is also somewhat defective. Even as a mental experiment, the analysis is too simple. The main use made of aggregate demand-and-supply curves, which usually follows, avoids some of the difficulties. That suggests to me that a different interpretation of aggregate demand and supply should be given in the first place, and it should use a quite different diagram that is sometimes found in textbooks in a different context.

In drawing a normal demand curve or supply curve for a firm or an industry, all changes that might occur, other than a change in the independent variable price, can properly be "locked in *caeteris paribus,*" and we then read from the curves the resultant changes in quantities. All changes other than price are "ruled out" in their effect, that is, the analysis abstracts from them. We need to inquire whether macro analysis can also take price as an independent variable and lock all other changes in caeteris paribus, that is, abstract from them in determining either the aggregate quantity demanded or the aggregate quantity supplied, as though aggregate demand and aggregate supply were independent of each other.

We can indeed treat demand conditions and supply conditions as independent of each other when analyzing a firm or an industry that does no advertising and is not oligopolistic. What a firm or an industry produces can be taken to have a negligible effect on its sales, because its employees are not a significant part of its market. Then the demand conditions and the supply conditions are the independent variables that govern. Actual money costs are related to the price level in the economy in general, but neither of these is expected to change by virtue of the decisions of the firm or industry. So it is demand conditions and supply conditions that contain, and so are, independent variables. Either demand or supply conditions can change independently of one another. So independent demand-and-supply curves can be drawn, varying only the price in order to see to see the quantity response. When the two curves are put together, both prices and quantities are determined simultaneously as dependent variables, dependent upon those demand-and-supply conditions.

But when a firm has some market power that it uses partly in advertising and especially when an industry is oligopolistic, demand-and-supply conditions are not entirely independent. That is the general case in our economy. When demand-and-supply conditions are somewhat interdependent, they cannot be taken as a basis for drawing independent demand-and-supply curves (see essay 11).

So we must examine the alternative explanation that textbooks give for drawing separate aggregate demand-and-supply curves as simple functions of price. The analysis should start with the economy in equilibrium and then introduce a change in some basic independent variable. Since the price level is not generally an independent variable, there is a difficulty in supposing that the price level could somehow be quite a lot higher or lower, and then talking about how quantities demanded or supplied could change independently of each other. Yet textbooks are doing that.

The reasoning is as follows. If the price level were presumed to be lower than it actually is, then the real value of the nation's money supply would be higher, and the wealth effect would result in a higher level of consumer spending, a major component of demand. It is argued also that the real value of government bonds would also be higher, with the same effects. There is an implicit assumption that liquidity preference was the same, so a higher real money supply would mean some of it would be used to purchase bonds, driving up their prices and lowering their yields. And so interest rates would be lower and real investment higher. A lower price level produces an increased quantity demanded since nothing offsets the higher consumption demand and higher investment demand. Aggregate supply is analyzed later.

In the above analysis it is implicitly assumed that even if the price level could be assumed to be lower than it is, the money supply would still be the same, as well as the government debt and everything else. None of these would be lower, but the price level could be assumed to be lower. It is not clear that, if the price level was lower, these other magnitudes would be what they are at the higher price level, but we shall ignore that for the present. If, then, the price level can be imagined to be lower and the other magnitudes not lower, what more is there to consider? It is not even clear what price index we should be talking about. Is it just the prices entered in the gross national product (GNP) price deflator, or should we be talking about all asset prices being lower or higher? In either case we might need to consider the behavior and effects of various assets and debts.

How might one imagine prices higher or lower and yet everything else the same? One might imagine price-makers managing to set prices higher than necessary, but not lower. One can imagine labor unions when at their most powerful getting wages higher than otherwise and forcing up the price level, or perhaps competition from the unemployed pushing wages down enough to get a lower price level than otherwise. But general price level increases and decreases are associated with the business cycle, so cannot be taken as imagined different price level differences with everything else the same. However, let us go along with the modern textbook assumption that price levels are higher or lower than they actually would be at an equilibrium or than they actually are at any given time, but all other economic magnitudes are not different, except for aggregate quantities demanded and supplied.

Is the wealth effect from a given nominal money supply at the lower price level all that needs to be considered? It increases consumption demand and the demand for government bonds if liquidity preference is unchanged, as implicitly assumed.

But what about other bonds? It is probably true that the higher asset value of government bonds matters more to people than the higher real liability of government. But can the same be said of other bonds and indeed of mortgage debt? At a lower price level, the real value of debt fixed in dollar terms is higher. Indeed may not the real burden of all other debt (debt other than government debt) matter more to the debtors than the real value of the assets to the asset holders? Imagining a very much lower price level, as suggested by the way the aggregate demand curve is drawn, might imply heavy overindebtedness for many if the volume of debt is that assumed at the beginning. Overindebtedness can even lead to bankruptcies and to creditors' reclaiming mortgaged properties of households and businesses. Security holders are often not as concerned about that as perhaps they should be.

Money is itself largely created by the monetization of private and public debt. Banks themselves would be in trouble if a lower price level meant many private debts could not be paid back to the banks.

A lower price level would not increase demand if the increased debt burdens, bankruptcies, and mortgage foreclosures outweighs the increase in the real value of money, as is likely. At the least it is not clear that there would be much slope, if any, to an aggregate demand curve that depended upon a wealth effect that was also necessarily combined with a debt effect.

Textbooks also say that one of the prices that would be lower if the price level were lower would be the interest rate, and that this would imply a higher real investment demand. That would be true if everything else remained the same. But would real investment demand increase even with the lower interest rate if the prices at which the resulting goods had to be sold was lower also? And would it be sufficient to raise the aggregate quantity demanded if the debt effect was more negative than the asset effect was positive?

Let us turn now to imagining a higher price level. According to the textbook reasoning, we see a lower real value of money and debt, so purchases (quantities demanded) would be lower. The lower real debt burden might be supposed to stimulate demand and offset the decline due to other factors. But it is not likely to have that strong an effect. One is still in debt, and although it will be easier to pay it off over time if one earns more dollars, if it costs more to live and earnings do not increase proportionately, one may not be able to meet even the somewhat easier debt payments. Earnings are implicitly assumed to remain the same whether the price level is lower or higher, else the conclusions would have to be modified. There is an asymmetry here: A higher debt burden may matter a lot and offset a positive wealth effect, but a lower debt burden is unlikely to matter much or offset a negative wealth effect.

Higher interest would also lower real investment demand if all else was the same. But if the price level is much higher, the higher price at which goods can be sold might offset the higher interest rate and induce a higher real investment demand. This might offset the fall in consumer demand.

A higher price level may or may not reduce the quantity demanded, and a lower price level may or may not raise it.

Which of the above considerations apply if one started more properly with changes in the nominal money supply? That is a legitimate policy variable. The difficulties just discussed do not appear. An increase in the money supply can have the same wealth effect as talked about before (inducing higher consumption, lower interest rates, and more real investment), but there is no increase in the burden of indebtedness as when the same effect is sought through a lower price level. The new equilibrium will come when the increased aggregate demand quantity has increased the demand for money as much as the supply of money increased. If increasing the money supply raised the price level, the new equilibrium would be defined the same way. Similarly a decrease in the nominal money supply would have a negative real wealth effect, reducing consumption, raising interest rates, and reducing real investment. So aggregate demand rises when the money supply increases and goes down when the money supply decreases.

We have yet to take into account the effects on aggregate quantity supplied of an increase in the money supply. Any increase in the quantity demanded will result in an increase in quantity supplied, and this in turn will increase quantity demanded further. This is the multiplier analysis. It is similar for a decrease in the money supply. All we need analyze further a little later is how much of the effect will be on output and how much on the price level. We need also to consider the other independent policy variable, fiscal policy. Its effects would be similar except that its direct impact on income is normally stronger than the indirect effect of changing the real value of money or even changing the liquidity of some other assets.

Let us next consider how some textbooks explain the aggregate supply curve, with price level the independent variable. The upward slope of the curve is explained by the fact that if the price level rose, profit margins would be higher, since input prices move up more slowly. When the price level falls, profit margins are pinched and output declines. This explains a rising supply curve.

Now this is introducing something new that was not considered when explaining the aggregate demand curve. This is not static but what might be called a historical dynamic model. It relies not upon imagining a different price level with much else unchanged. It relies upon a lag of part of the price level when a price level changes for some unexplained reason, or is imagined to change. What difference would it have made in the prior aggregate demand analysis if, when prices were imagined to be lower or higher, only finished-goods prices were different and all input prices, including especially wage rates, were not, at least for a time? A price-level decline would then produce an increase in purchases since wages and purchasing power did not decline, and the historical consequence would likely be that the price level would go up to where it was previously. Or a price-level increase unaccompanied by a wage-level increase would likely result in a decline in quantities demanded and the price-level increase would likely be rescinded.

However, let us return now to the textbook analysis of aggregate supply. If finished-goods prices rose but input prices did not, this would widen profit margins and increase the quantity supplied, according to textbooks. But is a widening of profit margins enough to increase the quantity of aggregate output supplied? Business incentives depend not only on margins but on markets, which is to say, on sales. And markets and sales depend not only on real asset values and debt burdens of households and businesses but especially upon household purchasing power, especially on labor income. If that did not increase at the same time and about as much as the finished-goods price level rose, the real volume of sales would fall off. It is doubtful if that could be offset by the reduced real burden of the debt. In any case, the debt-asset effect alone is clearly weaker than the income effect, especially since households do not have large holdings of liquid assets they could sell to finance larger purchases while continuing to service their debts, which are fixed in dollar terms. The real value of purchases is most likely to fall as the price level rises if wages do not rise. So the quantity supplied may fall if the price level rises and input prices do not rise. This is contrary to the textbook conclusion.

If finished-goods prices fall, profit margins are indeed squeezed, and outputs are cut rather quickly, lowering employment and hence income. The above analysis does not suggest that any effect on supply or demand will suffice to offset this, so the reduction in quantity supplied follows the price decline. There is an asymmetry here. A higher price level may not increase the quantity supplied, but a lower price will reduce the quantity supplied.

Now add the effect of interest-rate changes. The textbook argued that price-level changes would be accompanied by interest-rate changes in the same direction, and that this would change the rates of real investment. The latter would move inversely to the interest rate. A higher price level was supposed to raise interest rates and reduce real investment, but that would cast further doubt on the rising aggregate supply curve. A falling price level was supposed to decrease interest rates and raise real investment, but we know historically that real investment does not rise on the downswing of the cycle with falling price levels even though interest rates decline.

The analysis is not realistic in some other respects because rising or falling price levels are not independent variables but are usually the result of changes in the expected profitability of new real investments which drive the business cycle up and down. Prices and interest rates fall when the prospects for profitable investment have worsened so much that even with lower interest rates, real investment decreases. That characterizes much of the downswing of the business cycle. The investment curve moves to the left so much as to offset the interest-rate decline's impact on investment. Similarly, cyclical price-level increases raise interest rates, but these occur when increases in prospective investment profitability move the investment curve so much to the right as to more than offset the negative interest-rate effect on investment, so that real investment also increases. All this complicates the story of how quantities demanded or supplied and price-level changes are related. Over the business cycle, price level and output changes go up and down together.

The long and short of all this is that the standard-appearing aggregate demand-and-supply curves are easily manipulated in the usual fashion, but they do not have a satisfactory theoretical basis. As interpreted by students or as explained by the textbook, they should be thrown out. The curves are not independent. The textbooks latched on too quickly to reasoning that enabled them to draw normal-looking demand-and-supply curves, but a little further analysis would have made both those aggregate curves questionable.

The price level is not the independent variable to which the aggregate quantities demanded and supplied can be supposed to respond independently. Indeed aggregate quantity demanded and aggregate quantity supplied simply cannot be treated as independent of each other, for each is the major determinant of the other. According to Say's Law, supply creates its own demand, speaking in macroeconomic terms. This eliminated any degree of independence of the two, and it dealt with both supply and demand in the aggregate as quantities, not somehow independent schedules with price the independent variable for each.

Say's Law made so much sense that it took a long time for the error in it to be argued successfully by Keynes. But the error was that there could be a slippage at times between total production and total demand for it. There are leakages from and injections into the income stream that can result in short-run discrepancies between the total quantity of income produced and the quantity spent on that which was produced. So the bathtub theorem, dealing with imbalances between leakages and injections into the income stream, replaces Say's Law. The bathtub theorem says that the level of income remains constant when leakages from income and injections into income are equal; when leakages exceed injections, the income level is lowered; when injections exceed leakages, the income level rises. The analogy with a bathtub drain, spigot, and water level is obvious.

Most textbooks presenting the aggregate demand-and-supply curves use them for limited purposes which avoid many conceptual difficulties. The main use is to show what could move either of the curves and then indicate what the new equilibria would be. Discussion of any cycle comes later, if at all. The curves are assumed to be independent of each other, even though they are not. Yet much of what they say is all right because they rely upon the fact that although aggregate production and aggregate spending are the main determinants of each other, they can diverge somewhat for a time because leakages from the income stream and the injections into it need not be equal in the short run.

Most of the analysis runs in terms of changes in the quantity demanded causing changes in the quantity supplied and in the price level. The important thing is the analysis of what determines how much the price level is affected. From this point of view, no demand curve is needed. All that is needed is total spending as a single quantity, assuming whatever was the equilibrium price level at the beginning. A very different aggregate supply curve suffices. If total spending (demand) increases, this increases the aggregate quantity supplied (produced) (see Figure 1).

The price level as a dependent variable changes little or much depending upon where one is on the aggregate supply curve. The simplest example starts with the economy in a depression with a lot of unemployment at whatever the price level may be. That output–price combination may be plotted on Figure 1 somewhere in Phase 1. When recovery begins by injections exceeding leakages from the income stream, the aggregate quantity demanded increases and supply responds by moving to the right within Phase 1. Further stimuli to the economy can be thought of as moving farther to the right until the economy enters Phase 2. Then each increase in output increases the price level a little also. If stimuli continue, the farther we move to the right on the aggregate supply curve, the smaller the effect on output and the larger the effect on the price level in Phase 2. If stimuli continue, the economy enters Phase 3 where the entire effect is spent in raising the price level since short-run output capacity has been reached.

Most of the time the economy has levels of unemployment and

Figure 1. **Aggregate Supply Curve**

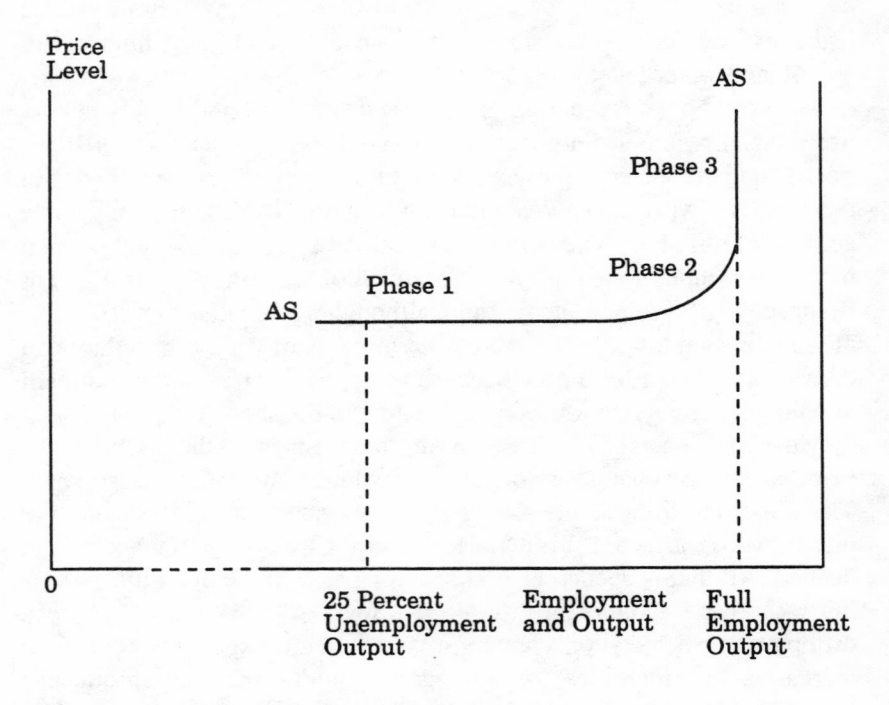

output in the intermediate range called Phase 2. In Phase 2, any increase in aggregate spending will have its effect divided between raising output and raising the price level. Now what determines how much the economy responds to the stimulus of increased effective demand (increased spending) by increases in the price level and how much by increases in real output? In general, the closer the economy is to "capacity" production, the bigger the price-level increase tends to be; and the more the stimulus increases output and employment, the greater the amount of unemployment. There have been attempts to show a quantitative relation between the slope of the resulting curve and the level of unemployment for some given period. Whatever relation is found, however, it should be obvious that the relation can change from time to time for any given point on the aggregate supply curve. What may be called technical and institutional factors may operate differently at different times with the same amount of unemployment and slack in the system.

It may be expected that the closer the economy moves to "capacity," the more industries will experience "bottlenecks," one of the reasons for more price rise in response to a stimulating increase in spending. But surely it will make a difference where the spending increases, and how many and which industries run into bottlenecks, and that may not be the same for a given amount of unemployment, from one recession or depression to the next. Bottlenecks may be shortages in capital capacity or lower productivity of additional labor hired or having to pay labor overtime or any combination of such factors.

As for institutional factors, the most important that can vary the results from time to time arise from business price policy and from labor union strength and policy. If labor unions take an improved economy as primarily a way to get more jobs, the result will be different from a situation in which they get no more jobs but take the improvement in the form of higher wages for those already employed. Clearly sometimes unions may be stronger than others, and thus their policy in this respect may make more difference or less. When there is a multiplier effect in response to a demand stimulus, business in general may sometimes take most of the improvement in an increase in sales volume, leading to production increases, and at other times to higher margins and price markups instead, or of course to various mixtures of the two strategies. The steepness of the curve at a given point is affected by labor and business decisions, which is to say that there will be a difference in how much a demand increase will raise prices and how much it will increase production.

Finally, the reconceived aggregate supply curve just discussed is a one-directional curve. The upswing of a business cycle may be described by the curve, but when a downswing follows, the economy does not ride back down the curve, with prices falling but no output drop at first. Rather, output tends to drop first, for reasons explained by various institutional semi-rigidities in prices and wages, and only after prolonged unemployment and recession are prices likely to drop much. The result is a sort of spiral in wages and prices over cycles, and an upward trend in the price level over time. Successive cycles move the Phase 3 line slowly to the right, representing increases in potential output arising from growth in productivity and in the volume of employed resources (capital and labor).

Reviewing now the analysis of the shift from the micro to the macro level in the treatment of demand and supply, the analysis led to dropping the aggregate demand curve, substituting the total volume of spending, and reinterpreting the aggregate supply curve. At the macro level, quantities supplied and quantities demanded are never even semi-independent but each is the major determinant of the other, and neither can be treated as an independent function of price. Changes in aggregate quantity supplied are ordinarily based upon expected changes in the aggregate quantity demanded, but innovation or other changes on the supply side can occur independently and produce changes in aggregate demand. We also have analyzed the things that determine some degree of accompanying change in the price level.

The textbooks discuss how a change in the aggregate demand or supply curve produces a new equilibrium. But this should be only a stepping-stone to discussing the somewhat irregular fluctuations in output that we often lump under the heading of business cycles. Economic historians can tell us that each "cycle" is somewhat unique, but economists ignore their uniqueness, however important the differences may sometimes be, to focus upon common features. Clearly changes in the rate of real investment are the main driving force in these cycles. Explanation of its changes is not simple. But students should learn that a cycle can be generated just by the combination of the multiplier and acceleration principles. First let us look at the downswing of a cycle.

Whenever aggregate demand falls short of supply because of leakages from the income stream, production falls, reducing income and spending, and that cuts production again. The economy does not usually unwind till there is no net saving. Often innovations generate increases in demand, which increase production, increasing income and spending and in turn production. If the innovation was a new consumer product, once each household that wants and can afford it has bought it, the industry that expanded to make that possible has to fall back largely on replacement demand. That drop in its production cuts income and spending and thus production again. More may be involved, but an inherent cycle easily perpetuates itself.

People have various beliefs about what other factors cause business cycles. Some believe that the cycles are due to changes in the relation between input and output prices. We have the curious situation where many people believe the unemployment in every downturn is due to wages' being too high, while some economists now believe it is due to the wages' being too low to induce labor to be willing to work. Neither theory has any relation whatsoever to reality. Anyone who thinks that the unemployment at the bottom of a business cycle is voluntary and could be cured if the unemployed were paid a little more is not aware of simple realities.

That cyclical unemployment is due to labor's pricing itself out of the market involves the same fallacy of composition that has been rejected in this essay. The demand-for-labor curve of a firm or an industry is downward sloping, and more labor will be employed at a lower wage rate because that will not affect sales, the employees being a negligible part of the market. But what is true of the part is not necessarily true of the whole. The aggregate demand-for-labor curve cannot lock in caeteris paribus aggregate sales in the economy. Total demand for goods and services will be the same if wage rates are cut only if employment increases proportionately to keep the aggregate wage bill the same. One has to assume demand for products to be the same to draw a demand curve for labor at all, so one cannot read off the curve how much more labor will be employed at a lower wage rate. Only one quantity of labor demanded satisfies the condition that quantity of product demanded remain the same for a given wage cut. Circular reasoning is involved in trying to draw the curve, and then only one point on the curve is any good unless it is a rectangular hyperbola. That would have to be assumed, not discovered. No one knows the shape of an aggregate demand-for-labor curve, nor how much it changes over time if one can be drawn at all. There is no way of knowing how much the quantity of labor demanded will change with a change in wage rates, because even though we know such wage rates will affect total purchasing power and business sales, there is no way to know how much that effect will be at any given time until we know how much business will change employment. Nobody can draw an aggregate demand curve for labor that can tell you that fact.

The labor unions, of course, never accepted the idea that an aggregate demand curve for labor in a recession was any good, but they engaged in a similar fantasy. They argued that if wages were increased, that would move any demand curve for labor to the right and increase employment. They assumed that purchasing power would be increased because the total wage bill would increase. But it would do that only if employment was not cut proportionately. They assume the answer they want—circular reasoning. No one can say confidently that a wage increase will always or ever increase labor income, reduce it, or leave it the same. We simply cannot generalize about how changes in wage rates will always change the quantity of labor employed. In some given instances, people with a good "ear to the ground" might make a good guess. But if the guess were publicized and believed widely enough, it might result either in actions that would make it a self-fulfilling prophecy or in widespread reactions that would invalidate it as prophecy.

It is clear to anyone who lives with the realities outside the text-books that there are various factors that can and do significantly influence the volume of employment, and that whatever they are, they operate chiefly through influencing the rate of real investment. If wage rates are one of the factors, we are unable to generalize about them.

The major direct variable in the whole picture is the expectation of return upon new real investment. Indeed there is no production except in anticipation of sales. Real investment is itself no simple function of any small set of underlying factors, so no simple theory of real invest-ment is worth much, though real investment is the engine whose changes drive the economy, increasing and decreasing income. The multiplier theory tells how much to expect income to change from a change in the rate of real investment if the price level does not change. The theory is more complicated when the price level changes also in Phase 2 of the aggregate supply curve. It can more easily be adapted to price-level change in Phase 3. Downhill applications are also difficult when the price level falls some.

Probably capital intensive-investment is a minor player in the whole game. More important has been capital-extensive investment when population has been growing. And Schumpeter's broad concept of innovation is probably most important of all. But there is no simple theory to explain that well, even from Schumpeter.

Now let us say a little about possible movements in the aggregate supply curve. It has already been mentioned that over time it slides to the right as there are increases in population (and labor force), or increases in capital and improvements in technology, both of which increase productivity. There may be increases in some resources and decreases in others that shift the curve to the right or upward or down-ward. Technology improvements may also lower costs and shift the curve downward.

Supply-side economics was conceived to shift the aggregate supply curve downward. Various measures were proposed to increase work incentives and lower production costs. Most important were tax cuts, especially for upper income groups. Most people's work hours were fixed, and the productivity effects of the measures were unclear. Along with doubling the military budget, supply-side economics was more effective in increasing demand than in shifting the supply curve down.

Then there is the inflation problem, which is sometimes a movement in Phase 2 or Phase 3 of the supply curve and sometimes an upward shift of the supply curve, or some of each. Sometimes demand exceeds supply, and demand-pull inflation may result if output cannot expand fast enough. It can be self-limiting or can escalate slowly or rapidly. This is moving to the right along the rising portion of the supply curve, or moving up its vertical portion. Sometimes wages are increased faster than productivity grows to produce cost-push inflation. Sometimes administered price inflation occurs when sellers increase prices. Inflation of these two types are represented by an upward shift of the supply curve. Finally, sectoral price inflation can develop when any of these three inflationary factors hits in important sectors of the economy. A sector can even be hit from outside the country, as by OPEC. The price level can rise due to these other factors independently of excess demand, though usually they are triggered by excess demand or accompanied by it, or some of them may come into play when moving into the region of the rising supply curve.

Let us conclude this discussion by some further methodological considerations. All efforts to explain economic phenomena by simple economic models necessarily abstract highly from reality. The only problems are whether they include all that is most important in relation to what they purport to explain, and whether they correctly show the relationships involved. Economists ordinarily suppose that wants, resources, and technology are the ultimate determining variables behind economic phenomena, and they treat these as changing independently of each other. To a large degree they are independent, but any one of them can be altered somewhat by effort in that direction. The direction of human efforts, as well as the amounts, can be explained partly endogenously by a good model, but only partly. So all four (wants, resources, technology, and effort) are only semi-independent determiners of our economy. It is very difficult indeed to model well the degrees of endogeneity involved at any given time or over time, more than it is to treat them all as exogenous and independent.

28. That Keynesian Revolution Controversy Again

Macroeconomics is now all post-Keynesian, but what that means concretely varies with economists. Popularly Keynes is now discredited by anti-Keynesians, although there is still some ongoing controversy. Here are some things to consider in evaluating the controversy that has followed ever since the publication of Keynes's *General Theory of Employment, Interest and Money* in 1936. A few things said in the preceding section may need to be repeated in this context.

The revolution in theory shifted the focus of attention from the price level to the level of employment and hence short-run real income, and it employed a different set of explanatory variables. Instead of explaining the price level by the quantity of money, four things allegedly determine the level of employment and real income. Three of the determinants are psychological variables: the propensity to consume (and hence to save), the expected returns on new real investment, and the preference for liquid assets; and the fourth, the "real" money supply, is a policy-determined variable.

This theory would have caused a tempest in the academic teapot but not much public commotion except that the consequent policy recommendation for the depression was government deficit spending. That was widely regarded, especially in the business and financial world, as both unsound and antibusiness, hence dangerously revolutionary. Without repeating here more than necessary of the typical textbook exposition of macro theory, the following will attempt to call attention to, and take a position on, a few aspects of the controversy.

At its simplest level, the Keynesian theory says that output (real national income Y) is a multiple of autonomous injections (J) into the income stream ($Y = kJ$) (the multiplier is k). The injections are spending to produce real capital equipment (I) and the vertical intercept of the consumption function. The consumption function is based upon simple observations: that people's incomes can be too low for them to save, and that above that level increases in income are partly saved. And, given the strength of our desire to consume, the amount we save or spend on consumption depends primarily upon our income. Those not very revolutionary propositions suffice to show that the multiplier (k) is the reciprocal of the marginal propensity to save. All that should be familiar.

The real investment rate (I) in the above formulation can then be

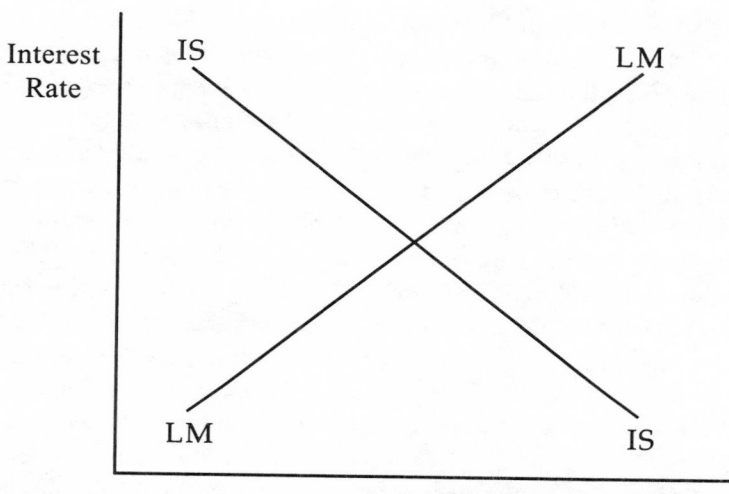

Saving and investment are equal at all points on the IS curve.

The demand and supply of money are equal at all points on the LM curve.

The equilibrium levels of interest and national income are found where the IS and LM curves cross.

explained on the ground that business will undertake any such investment expected to yield a return equal to or higher than the rate of interest, and that the higher the interest rate, the fewer investments expected to yield that much. Nothing revolutionary here either, though clearly this does not explain the important factors that affect the rate of investment other than the interest rate, and the usual economist's simplification in speaking of "the" interest rate needs to be understood as speaking of the level of interest rates.

The extent to which we wish to keep our financial assets in purely liquid form is then said to be an inverse function of the interest rate, and the equilibrium interest rate is determined by that psychological preference and the existent amount of pure liquidity (i.e., the money supply), both demand and supply of liquidity considered in real terms. Again nothing revolutionary, though this isolates only one of the pairs of factors that can affect interest.

The above-mentioned bathtub theorem puts these four things together. At equilibrium, saving and investment must be equalized, as must the demand and supply of money. It is shown (by the IS curve in the IS-LM diagram) that interest and income would have to move inversely for saving and investment to be equalized, given the shapes of the normal consumption function and marginal efficiency function (showing profitable rates of investment for different expected rates of return and interest rates). For the demand for money to remain equal to a fixed supply of money, interest rates and income would have to vary in the same direction (as shown by the LM curve in the same diagram). Obviously there is then only one combination of interest rate and income level that produces equilibrium given the three psychological factors and the policy-determined real money supply, and it is shown diagrammatically in the intersection of the IS and LM curves.

There is nothing much to quarrel with when it comes to saying that each of those four factors is important in determining short-run output and that each tends to affect it in the direction implied by the Keynesian theory.

Yet the classical view was that the economy automatically produced a full employment level of output, some basing this upon Say's Law, which Keynes said was blindly assumed and must be repudiated. For Say's Law, it was indeed competition that was supposed to maintain full employment. So unemployment had to be attributed, when it existed, to lack of sufficient competition. The position taken in this essay is that oligopoly, our main form of monopoly power, will distort resource allocation, when not based on scale economies, but it will not of itself reduce employment in the aggregate. Insufficient competition in labor markets and in the savings market requires more extended discussion.

It is still contended in some quarters that unemployment, alleged by Keynesians to be due to insufficient aggregate demand, can be cured simply by competition in the labor market cutting the wage level sufficiently. The simplest formulation of the argument runs into the old enemy, the fallacy of composition. It is said that just as the micro demand curve for labor is downward sloping, so is the aggregate demand curve for labor, so a sufficient cut in the wage rate will generate full employment. But the demand curve for labor for a single firm or industry assumes legitimately that the demand for the product will not be affected by a wage cut by the firm, since the employees are an insignificant part of the firm's or industry's market. The same cannot be said at the macro level. Aggregate demand for output cannot be said to remain unchanged unless purchasing power is unaffected when there is a general wage cut. But total purchasing power will be unchanged only if the increase in employment is enough to make the total wage bill the same as before. One would have to know that just that much of an increase in employment would result from a wage cut in order to draw an aggregate demand-for-labor curve in the first place. The argument for the wage cut cannot be based on a curve for which one must already know that there will be a certain outcome in order to draw the curve. To draw the desired conclusion from the curve involves circular reasoning. The curve cannot be drawn at the aggregate level without assuming the answer it is supposed to provide the proof of.

Labor unions never accepted the reasoning, alleging that employment could be increased if the demand curve was moved to the right by increasing wages. This suffers from the same sort of circular reasoning. It assumes without basis that a rise in wage rate will not result in a reduction in employment so great that the aggregate wage bill would fall instead of rise. The union would have to know what would happen to employment if wages were raised in order to show that the demand curve would move in the direction desired, so one cannot use such movement to prove what would happen to employment.

What can be demonstrated to be the effect on employment of a wage cut? Alas, nothing can be proven from an aggregate demand curve for labor since that involves holding constant, as the wage rate changes, things that cannot legitimately be assumed to remain constant. Indeed economists cannot safely generalize about the result of wage cuts or increases. In earlier business downswings there were sometimes downward price and wage movements which tended to reinforce each other. A cumulative downward wage–price spiral might be the outcome of general wage cuts to cure unemployment, whether the cuts resulted from sufficient competition in the wage market or from government dictation. It is not entirely clear either how sufficient competition could be introduced or how constitutionally a policy of a general wage cut could be undertaken. Busting labor unions, which cover only a minority of labor would supposedly do it, according to antiunionists, but there is room to doubt that this would suffice even if it could be done and done legitimately. Altogether it would seem that we should have heard the last of the talk that competition in the labor market or across-the-board wage cuts can be shown by an aggregate demand curve for labor to be the cure for unemployment due to insufficient aggregate demand for goods and services.

Then what about the classical view that might be taken to lie behind Say's Law that competition in the financial sector of the economy would cure unemployment. Classical economists recognized that income saved was not creating a demand for products and hence not for the labor to make them. But their notion was that savings were returned to the income stream through being spent on capital goods. What guaranteed that savings would be invested, leading to alteration in the allocation of labor between producing consumer goods and capital goods, but not altering the total demand for labor, was the interest rate. If saving exceeded investment, creating a problem, competition would force the interest rate down until all savings were being invested. If competition was insufficient to make this happen, it should be a simple matter for monetary policy to force down the interest rate. Recessions and depressions could thus be either prevented or cured by simple monetary policy. One must ask why, then, business cycles were not cured or prevented long ago. Did not interest rates fall during business downswings? Of course they did, but that did not produce the cures that the old theory claimed.

The Keynesian analysis implies that savings and investment can sometimes not be equalized at full employment by interest-rate changes because of the low interest elasticity of the savings function and the investment function at times. The classical analysis assumed that the savings and investment curves were usually both relatively flat, whereas when a decline in interest rates does not do the job it must be because the curves are relatively steep. When those functions are represented by curves that intersect below the x-axis after a sharp move to the left of the investment curve, no positive rate of interest can equate saving and investment, only a drop in the income level can do so. This does not mean that lower interest rates do not help by reducing the deflationary gap, but it means monetary policy alone cannot cure a serious recession or depression caused by a large leftward shift of the investment curve, that is, by a substantial worsening in the prospects of new real investment.

All this is to explain why the classical economic prescription, more competition, is not in general sufficient to prevent or cure the downswing of the business cycle. Indeed the cure of any serious mass unemployment must look for increases in aggregate demand through reductions in leakages or increased injections. Starting with the foreign trade balance, the prospects of success here are very poor partly because other nations can employ the same tactic at the same time with a shrinking of trade the main outcome. Exhorting people to save less and spend more in the circumstances of falling employment is not good advice and not likely to be effective. Since a decline in real investment is the usual cause of downswings in the economy, one might exhort business to invest more, but this too will not work because it is the prospects of profitable investment that have worsened and caused the unemployment, and exhortation does not alter these investment prospects. That leaves the balance between taxes and government expenditures as the only place to change aggregate demand. A government deficit can obviously offset the excess of saving over investment and on an appropriate scale can restore full employment.

This is the Keynesian policy revolution, held to be antibusiness although it is the only way in some circumstances to increase business sales in the aggregate. In another respect the revolution amounts to staggering deficit spending so as to stabilize the economy instead of reinforcing the business cycle. Historically governments (all levels together) have undertaken bond issues for public works in boom times when resources were scarce, and governments have cut back expenditures and raised taxes in depression. The Keynesian revolution would time deficits to offset, not worsen, the business cycle. Reasons can be given for preferring tax cuts to increasing government expenditures to create a deficit, or vice versa, at times, but the desired effects on employment can be obtained by appropriate amounts either way. It has often been pointed out that a downswing in the economy generates a government budget deficit automatically. But while this helps cushion the downswing, the automatic stabilizer, as it is called, is not itself sufficient in magnitude to produce recovery.

Revolutions produce counterrevolutions, so there has been a continuous series of attacks on Keynesian theory and policy by some economists and others. The attacks go beyond making improvements upon the initial theory and attempt to discredit and destroy it. One of the first basic attacks tried to resurrect the wage cut as a depression remedy by claiming that a decline in wages and prices, while keeping the money supply constant, could so increase people's real wealth by increasing the real value of the money supply that people would spend enough more to restore full employment. This was called the Pigou Effect. Never mind that the huge fall in price levels necessary to have this effect on money holders would also produce a massive wave of bankruptcies of businesses that had fixed debts that could not be serviced at drastically lowered price levels. Yet there was not the protest of this as antibusiness as there was against a Keynesian policy that would instead increase business sales. Rationality did not characterize the controversy over Keynes. Insofar as the wage-cut policy could work via the wealth effect, it was doing so by reducing the demand for money relative to a fixed supply. This was simply a poor way, with serious side effects, to get what an easy money policy could get without bad side effects, simply by increasing the money supply relative to the demand for money. That would reduce interest rates. We have already discussed the limited value of monetary policy when saving and investment curves are rather steep. And more liquidity may not increase spending in a recession.

Then there was the charge that financing a government deficit inevitably raised interest rates, which would cut back private real investment, leaving total spending unchanged. This "crowding out," as it was called, is easily avoided by open market purchases by the Federal Reserve to check any rise in interest rates by financing the deficit with new money. The ongoing controversy about the interest elasticity of the demand for money is not worth much since the multiplier is clearly greater when new money finances the deficits. Then the claim was made that it was only the increase in the money supply that produced the effect. Something has been said above about the limited effectiveness of monetary policy alone. Here a question may be raised about the relative effectiveness of monetary policies that merely increase dollars in exchange for government securities (near money) on the one hand, and on the other hand policies that increase the money supply to finance increased production, and thus, directly increase people's after-tax incomes resulting from a government deficit. The latter clearly has the greater effect.

The latest attack on Keynes is misnamed the rational expectations approach. It is important, but nothing new, to say that all decisions are made in terms of expected future values of relevant variables, though current or historical values may give some clues. What is new is calling it rational for people to assume that any government deficit spending, even in a depression, will produce only inflation, leading all labor to react by raising wage rates so much that no change in the level of employment results. It is simply not a rational expectation at all to suppose that any fiscal stimulus, unlike any other stimulus, will, at a time when there is even recessionary unemployment, only raise the general price level.

To be sure, if business's reaction to the increase in sales that the deficit spending generates is to cut back investment by an equal amount, employment will not increase. Or if business foresees a rise in sales resulting from the deficit spending and decides to raise profit margins and prices instead of increasing sales volume, the effect of the deficit on employment can be defeated. Or it is at least conceivable that in some recession, all labor already employed might demand and get such substantial wage increases that it might raise prices enough to absorb the increased spending without increasing employment. Or if an accompanying easy-money policy creates similar fears of inflation despite the room for noninflationary output expansion, monetary-fiscal policy can be rendered ineffective, and the economy can remain stuck, perhaps for a long time, at whatever level of unemployment may develop at times. But there is nothing rational about an expectation that policies that increase business sales with lots of slack in the economy must be self-defeating and produce only price inflation. Only irrational expectations can produce reactions to monetary-fiscal policies appropriate for recessionary periods that would render such policies ineffective in reducing cyclical unemployment. Recent stagflation presents a new type of problem for which neither classical nor Keynesian remedies suffice. This will be discussed later along with inflation.

The concept of a natural level of unemployment got reinterpreted in the course of this controversy. It had always been supposed that economic change plus freedom to look for different jobs would result in some percentage of the labor force being temporarily unemployed at all times, though not the same people all the time. Now it appears as though whatever the percentage that is unemployed at a given time, that is alleged to be the new natural rate, and it is claimed that it would be inflationary to try to reduce it by monetary-fiscal policy. This is nonsense when there is a lot of unemployment and slack in the economy. Indeed there has not even been much effort to reduce unemployment to older normal levels by proper retraining and improvements in the job market and better matching of skills to existing job vacancies.

A politically popular anti-Keynesianism in the 1980s went by the name of "supply-side economics." The idea was that we should not increase output and employment by increasing demand but by measures alleged to increase supply in other ways. The favorite was reducing taxes, especially on upper-income groups, in order to induce people to work more and harder and produce more and to induce business to invest more. This was to be done without creating a deficit due to the proposition that the economy was on the downward sloping side of the Laffer curve, hence tax revenues would increase at lower tax rates. That proposition was wrong, and it was wrong that lower tax rates would result in people's generally working harder and longer to increase output. The increase in spending that resulted from the tax cut came initially, as Keynesians said, from increased consumer spending. A large further stimulus came from the doubling of the military budget. The supply-side effects were nil. Students should, however, read the unreconstructed supply-siders to see how they now defend their position, including downplaying the significance of government deficits that were formerly the center of anti-Keynesianism.

The purpose of the above comments on the controversy over Keynes is to help offset the tendency of recent textbooks to be overinfluenced by the anti-Keynesians because that is what is now more popular, even in academic circles. Hence there is no need to elaborate on the modifications that have necessarily been made in the earlier textbook Keynesian models. One major modification in the simple multiplier was implied in what has been said about the division of a stimulus between a price change and an output change, a modification that rational expectationists carried too far in denying any output change, except (for some) a very temporary change. More has been learned about short- and long-run consumption functions. The monetary analysis confined to the bond-money alternative was oversimplified. But the IS-LM analysis permits all interest theories to be included. The major shortcoming in the investment analysis was not as easily remedied because any realistic investment function appears to be extremely complex. It is hard to generalize about the relative strengths of various factors in it, and the function may not be very stable. Indeed it is the cyclical shifts in the marginal efficiency of investment curve that explains most changes in the rate of real investment, not movements along the curve. For some time the interaction between multiplier and accelerator principles, and more recently the critical significance of their magnitudes, has provided some additional insight into cycles. Indeed the major significance of macroeconomic analysis should be to provide more insight into business fluctuations. Neither textbook static Keynesian models nor anti-Keynesianism can do this, though the former provides a useful stepping-stone.

The recent assumption of market clearing, the darling of many economists now, yields a nice classical model of an economy. But it has not an ounce of realism. Clearly the notion that all markets, including the labor markets, clear by price-level movements is nonsense, and the disequilibrium paths when they don't clear are significant.

Monetary-fiscal policy to deal with recession cannot be written off by choosing assumptions that in effect preclude it. Government simply has a responsibility for full employment when investment is insufficient.

The problem in such cases could be incentives or markets. With the excessive inequality that now exists, and with CEOs writing their own pay and bonuses at levels that clearly have nothing to do with their marginal productivity or anything else but their greed, disposable-income incentive is not the problem. At times, markets in the aggregate are clearly not strong enough to call for new investment on a scale to offset all savings. Yet business and many economists always call for more saving, as though a shortage of saving was the problem, not a shortage of real investment. There is always the possibility of innovations' stimulating investment, but once the market for an innovation has been satisfied and demand drops back to replacement levels, more innovation is needed but may not be forthcoming.

Meanwhile there are serious needs going unmet because of the extensive poverty that prevails—inadequate purchasing power of the working poor and others to meet their obvious needs. A less unequal distribution of income and a cure of the poverty problem would provide very substantial increases in market demands, and thus also help cure the problem of unemployment as well as the inequity problem. Living wages even at the bottom of the income scale would help maintain a higher level of demand even after deficiencies were made up, and thus tend to maintain a higher level of employment of minorities in central cities. It just might even reduce crime rates and associated expenditures, such as for prisons. But housing for the poor does not pay, so government builds prisons instead. That is the "practical" outcome of different economic theories, built upon different assumptions.

29. The Welfare State

The Great Depression also led to the initiation in this country of what has been described as the welfare state. Unemployment insurance, social security, Medicare and Medicaid, and Aid to Families with Dependent Children (AFDC) are the heart of it. These are largely attempts to use government to provide some assistance to people who are victims of economic insecurity. As such, it has been a substantial success story.[22] It is not supposed that people do not try to make some provision themselves, but that additional help may be needed. Certainly those in poverty are not able to provide for insecurity and not all lower-middle-class people can. Indeed anyone can be hit by medical bills that only the wealthy can protect themselves against. Our social security system is far from providing adequate protection against economic insecurity beyond what individual saving can provide.

Provision for old age in the social security legislation was expected to be supplemented by private saving and pensions from one's employer, and provision for widows from private life insurance. But as businesses fail, pensions disappear, and not everyone is able to stay with a single business long enough to have an adequate pension. Indeed it is not clear why business should be saddled with the payment of pensions to employees for life after their retirement. Pensions might better be financed through social security than be imposed on business and sometimes on nonbusiness employers.

But the whole welfare state concept has been under attack from the political right wing. AFDC has had problems that need correcting, but the question is at what age of her children a mother should be required to work, and what if there are no jobs to be had.

There have also been problems of escalating costs in the Medicare system that require attention. There was discussion during the Clinton administration about how to improve the medical and medical insurance systems so as to control costs, and, more important, to provide everybody with medical insurance. But though the issues to be dealt with are complex, they were not discussed rationally. Political posturing and press publicity completely mixed up the public and defeated any attempt to deal effectively with the problem.

The whole safety net system to prevent people from being impoverished through no fault of their own needs extensive discussion, but this is not the place for it. Private insurance plays an important role in dealing with economic insecurity, but needs to be supplemented by well-designed social security measures. The attempt to return parts of the social security system to the states is a dishonest attempt to weaken the system, as it is well known that at the state level, every state legislature is played off against others to keep taxes down under threat of business leaving the state. It would seem that real issues surrounding economic insecurity such as these might find a more ample treatment in the economics textbooks.

College students should at least be helped to see how incredible it is that politicians can get away with cutting a deficit by proposals to cut the safety net budget while keeping safe and even increasing a military budget that was bloated by a cold war that has ended against a Warsaw Pact that cannot be revived. Even the Center for Defense Information has shown that the military budget could be safely cut to about $100 billion. A reformed and extended social security system could readily be afforded if a small part of the bloat in the military budget was all that was sacrificed. When will we talk sense in terms of the possible gains in economic security that we are now giving up to keep an inexcusably large military establishment? Let's get our textbooks down to facing the big issues that daily affect people's real security.

30. Inflation and Stagflation

Standard textbooks generally explain adequately the effects of inflation which lead some people to oppose it and some to favor it. Books distinguish different types of inflation and the consequences of employing monetary-fiscal policies to combat different types of inflation. The political arena and the news media do not do a satisfactory job of helping the public understand what they need to understand without reading the textbooks. In general, politicians choose their own whipping boys for any inflation, especially blaming the other political party or labor unions or occasionally big business. There is little explanation of how the mix of inflationary factors in the United States has changed almost from year to year since World War II. Nor is there much publicity given to admissions by some persons in both Democratic and Republican administrations that their administration policies settled for higher and longer unemployment to help break the back of inflation.

The classical versus Keynesian controversy is less acute with respect to inflation. The usual charge is that Keynesianism is only depression economics and has nothing to say about inflation. It was certainly developed to explain and deal with depression, but the theory has applicability to demand-pull inflation that is stronger medicine than is politically popular, namely tight monetary-fiscal policy. When that type of inflation rears its head, the proper charge is not against Keynesian theory or policy but against the unwillingness and failure of politicians to apply it at all or to apply it sufficiently strongly.

The real rub is that a tightening of monetary-fiscal policy has been applied to deal with other types of inflation, other than excess demand inflation, with the result of increasing unemployment. When inflation is cost-push rather than demand-pull, or when business-pricing policies lead to general inflation, or even when we have prices rise for any reason in some key sector of the economy, the attempt to cure it by tight monetary-fiscal policy will fail to stop it but will create substantial unemployment. Antitrust enforcement can be applied to sellers inflation, though that will not be a sufficient remedy. Cost-push is usually wage-push. More about that and about sectoral inflation shortly.

Few textbooks still insist on an old classical view that the general price level is not changed by any changes in relative prices, the theory presuming that increases in prices in one sector of the economy would "naturally" be offset by decreases elsewhere, rather than spreading and generating a rise in the price level. OPEC's effect on the price level made it hard to maintain that old idea. But the price-level effects of OPEC are underestimated by those who simply calculate the share, direct or even indirect, of oil in GNP. OPEC hurt our standard of living both by such price increases and by worsening the nation's terms of trade. People tried to offset the higher price of oil and protect their standard of living by wage and salary increases. Such an attempt initiates a wage-price spiral, and where it ends is not readily predictable. OPEC triggered such a spiral.

Classical economics can properly be taken to warn us that a country will have continuous inflation if wages and salaries generally increase faster than average productivity increases. Pay rates used to be fairly well defined for each job; increase would occur for length of service, or go with promotions, but there was no annual pay raise for everybody. As productivity increases, the price level could slowly decline if annual increases in wages were avoided or if average wage increases were less than average productivity increases. It is the relatively new tendency in the United States to expect and get annual increases in pay unrelated to and exceeding average productivity increases that creates an underlying rate of inflation. One problem with even a slowly rising price level is that it slowly taxes away one's saving for retirement. The purchasing power of accumulated savings would be cut in half in a dozen years by a 6 percent annual rate of inflation. The other major problem with inflation is the danger of the rate's increasing and even getting out of hand, especially if people try both to catch up with it and to outpace it, and especially if government policies are inadequate or inappropriate.

Stagflation presents a real dilemma for macroeconomic policy for which there is no simple and adequate remedy, let alone a palatable one. A macro policy to cut unemployment might increase inflation in this situation; the opposite macro policy to reduce inflation would likely add to unemployment. It is clear that in stagflation the inflation is not due to excess demand or there would not be the substantial unemployment which is at least to some extent a reflection of inadequate aggregate demand. Insofar as it is the latter, what seems to be called for is a stimulative macro policy accompanied by something that prevents an inflationary response, something that limits price increases to cost increases and limits pay increases to average productivity increases. That was the idea behind the Walter Heller wage-price guideposts and behind TIPS (tax-based incomes policies) ideas. The failure of some European incomes policies is partly attributable to lack of advance understanding and agreement with respect to how much profits should be allowed to increase with recovery from low employment levels. This is an area where further experience might clarify the conditions for success. An unsolved problem for any such approach is the tendency to freeze the wage pattern and blunt any attempts to rectify what may be unjustifiable relative rates of pay. When there is a lot of unemployment, inflation has to be due to business price policies, so-called sellers inflation. The press sometimes carries stories that business is just waiting for a chance to raise prices. If it doesn't wait, we get a bigger secular inflation trend than necessary. If guideposts do not restrain it, TIPS may be necessary, though that is not a desirable long-run policy.

We used to think that inflation was primarily a problem of other countries' unstable governments. It now appears as though the United States has the inflation problem too. It tends to have sellers inflation, and it regularly violates the classical dictum that pay increases must not exceed average productivity increases. The custom has become annual pay increases in almost every job, with everyone trying to get as much as they can. The inequity is that those who push less or are weaker bargainers get left behind and do more than their share of suffering from the inflation. The problem is how to change the business price and the wage customs in such a manner that prices are more stable. Import competition may have given us only temporary relief from this inflation problem.

31. Rules versus Discretion in Macroeconomic Policy

There is a broader issue with respect to macroeconomic policy. It is apparent that not all errors in economic policy are attributable to the ignorance of politicians or their susceptibility to undue influence from special interests. Competent economists disagree, and advice is sometimes mistaken. This has led one school of thought to argue for minimizing discretionary powers in macroeconomic policy. Fiscal policy is to be left to the automatic stabilizers. Monetary policy is to be restricted to the execution of a fixed rule: Expand the money supply at a fixed annual rate of perhaps 3 percent to finance slow growth of total output. The alternative, to give monetary authorities power to use their discretion with respect to the use of their monetary tools, is said to risk mistakes that may make things worse rather than better. It seems to be overlooked that the rule would not really eliminate day-to-day discretion, but remove discretion as to proximate monetary targets.

The best case that can be made for such a stance is the finding that there are several lags of variable length involved, so discretionary policy may produce an effect at the wrong time. There are lags between economic changes and their reporting and recognition, between recognition and decisions as to what to do, between decisions and their execution, and between execution and economic effects. Yet it is obvious that the economy is not automatically stabilized by any macro policy that is fixed and does not vary with conditions. The only question is whether such a policy likely results in worse or better outcomes than a discretionary policy does. Whatever the record in the past may be, that is not conclusive, since it can be presumed that experience teaches us to do better in the future. To be sure, management should always be assumed to be less than perfect. With hindsight it may always appear to have been poor management to some extent. Management's critics say that trusting management is trusting luck as much as management's limited wisdom. But the critics of a fixed rule say that is trusting luck entirely without recourse to any learning or wisdom.

It is clear that some people are psychologically unwilling to accept the results of a fixed rule. That really means accepting macroeconomic conditions, however bad they may become, rather than trying to take their destiny in their own hands to some extent. They prefer to do that even at the risk of making things worse, because they are confident they can (and are determined to) learn from their mistakes. Other people appear to be psychologically unwilling to trust to human discretion in such matters lest that might make matters worse. They know the economy will dish up unsatisfactory conditions at times that they could have tried to do something about. But they are afraid to give anyone discretionary power to try to do something that could make things worse rather than better. This difference in people's attitudes may underlie the most basic differences in orientation to macroeconomic policy issues.

The International Economy

32. International Economic Relations

Recently there has been more attention to the importance of international economic relations. To study them, students need background in both micro and macro; but when the topic is put at the end of the book, instructors may fail to get that far in the course. There is a problem in any case if the books don't provide enough tie to the real international relations issues that are not just a matter of the theory of comparative advantage. One may get a discussion of protectionism as against free trade principles, but one may get little if any indication of the respects in which the cold war distorted international trade and investment, little if anything on the background of and nature of the third world demands for a New International Economic Order, little if anything on the conflict over the Common Agricultural Policy of the European Economic Community, little on the complex factors in the U.S. quarrel with Japan, and little on the complex sets of factors leading to the breakdown first of the gold standard and then of the Bretton Woods System. Having any real understanding of international economic relations is simply not reducible merely to understanding the principle of comparative advantage and the present nonsystem in international exchange rate determination.

As for comparative advantage, despite efforts to distinguish it from absolute advantage, students typically do not learn why trade would pay even if a country was in some sense more efficient in every line of production than competitors, or how a country could still trade profitably even if it was less efficient in every line than any foreign country. The clue, of course, is that the degree of a country's superiority or inferiority in different lines would not be, indeed could not be, exactly the same; hence it would pay to specialize in producing and exporting those things in which its advantage was greatest or its disadvantage least.

The student who is paying attention to the discussions, outside the textbook, of the decline of U.S. international competitiveness may be puzzled as to what to make of the matter. This requires some discussion and clarification of issues and implications. One might gather from what one can read elsewhere that our decline is proven by statistics that show that the U.S. share of total world trade has been falling since early post–World War II years. To some extent this change is a natural consequence of economic progress elsewhere in the world. It took time after World War II for Europe and Japan to achieve the role in world trade that reflected their potential competitiveness. And the third world, especially some of the so-called newly industrializing countries, are naturally going to enter the international economy on an increasing scale. The United States may indeed be better off as a result of such developments, rather than worse off, which is what is inferred from figures on our share of world trade. There is no ground for saying that the United States should have some particular share of total world trade, or for saying that the share we have at some particular time should never decline, or for saying that any decline is because we are failing at something instead of that others are improving economically, perhaps even relative to us.

Some people in this country seem to think that we are somehow supposed to be the best at everything, and that it is a terrible thing if any other country catches up in some lines or surpasses us in some. That can be taken in foreign quarters to be objectionable American vanity and arrogance. It is not very becoming to take the attitude that we must always be better in everything and that we must always be better off than every other country. We would not be hurt but probably would benefit if most people of other countries were able to enjoy the same standard of living that we enjoy. Mutually beneficial trade would increase.

It would be better if, instead of worrying about others' relative position, we concerned ourselves, as we legitimately can, with whether we are living up to our own potential in terms of economic progress. Whether that means we Joneses stay ahead relatively or not should not be the issue. Indeed we ought to welcome others' catching up, and if others get ahead we have nothing to be ashamed of if we are living up to our own best potentials.

That we are perhaps not doing so is the real issue. But that is not to be judged by our share of international trade. Then perhaps something can be learned in this respect by finding out why some former export industries are now import industries. It may be that we are doing all right but other countries have developed a comparative advantage. Comparative advantages do not stand still forever; for one thing, they may shift because some country does not progress according to its own potential, or because some other countries have indeed finally achieved their own true potential. The focus should be on whether we are doing as well as should be expected, accepting whatever this means in terms of changes in international trade. A trade change does not of itself necessarily mean we are not doing what we could, though it could reflect such failure.

From such considerations, let us turn to the basic core of international relations textbooks, the theory of trade. Students are sometimes confused by textbooks that present various modern theories of international trade and then criticize each on some grounds, such as that some trade does not fit the theory, or provide empirical data to show that it does not hold up well overall. It is as though a theory was no good if it did not explain all international trade. In the nature of the case, that is impossible; some trade needs to be explained by one theory and some by another theory, and that should be made clear instead of sounding as though each theory had serious flaws.

Whatever the treatment, what it all adds up to in the textbooks is an overwhelming theoretical case for the advantages of free trade. One might well wonder why, if that is the case, tariffs have been one of the staples of political controversy throughout U.S. history. The reasons should be made more explicit. To be sure, ignorance or misunderstanding of the economics probably played an important part. But at least as important is the fact that there is a conflict of interest involved. The primary conflict is not between this country and other countries; trade is in their mutual interest, and the terms of trade that divide the gains between them is a matter of demand and supply. Efforts to alter the terms will be discussed below. The basic conflict of interest involved in foreign trade policy is a conflict within each country. It is easy to identify those who gain and those who lose by reduced protectionism and expanding trade. The winners are consumers in general, exporters, import-using producers, and the businesses involved in the mechanics of trading (shippers, and so on). The losers are import-competing producers. Consumers are unorganized, and import-competing producers have historically often been organized for lobbying Congress for protection better than other producer interests such as exporters, have been organized for freer trade.

Protectionist interests make it sound as though foreign producers are generally dumping their goods in our markets to the detriment of domestic producers and this country as a whole. The term "dumping" is loosely used, and there can be cases of predatory dumping that are not in the national interest, though price discrimination in our favor is not in general such a case. But the argument over our importation of steel from foreign sources, unless involving predatory dumping, is a conflict between U.S. producers of steel and U.S. firms who prefer to buy foreign steel and insist on their right and opportunity to do so. The scrap is not between two countries but between two sets of businesses in this country. And that needs to be made perfectly clear.

Though in general we benefit whenever we can get something cheaper from abroad, we can properly object to predatory dumping, and every country needs protection against the practice, though it is less common than alleged. Governmental subsidy of exports raises another issue. If we could count on a foreign government permanently subsidizing our consumption of their exports, we should be delighted, but such help can't be counted upon continuously, so import-competing firms complain and seek protection against any foreign subsidy of their competitors. U.S. government policies promote our export businesses in general in a number of ways, and this also amounts to a subsidy. But many governments do this, so the problem is not subsidy as such but differences over what constitutes an acceptable subsidy and what is to be considered unfair. There are sticky questions relating to such things as tax rebates. Direct subsidy of a specific export usually raises objections. Yet much of our own agricultural exports are possible only by government subsidy since their domestic prices are supported at above market levels.

The aspect of international economics that students as citizens will likely meet most directly involves the question as to what particular protectionism, if any, to support. Alleged adverse effects of international trade on wage rates and employment are of greatest concern, and textbooks deal with these. Typically it is shown that whatever the relative wage levels of countries, exchange-rate adjustments take them into account and in effect offset the differences. The result is that each country necessarily has a comparative advantage in some things and can trade profitably. The low-wage countries cannot undersell the high-wage countries in everything. It can be added that the resulting trade does tend to raise wage levels in export industries and check their rise in import-competing industries in each country. Resources tend to shift away from the latter industries, while others shift to the former, thus tending to raise the average wage level in each country, since relatively more labor becomes employed in the higher-wage export industries. This is how labor gets some of the benefit of trade, while the consumer gets it in lower prices of whatever is imported.

The employment effect of trade is more complicated. The level of employment in a country in the long run is not determined by whether it has a high volume of international trade or whether it is economically self-sufficient. International trade determines only the allocation of labor as between lines in which a country has a comparative advantage and those in which it has a comparative disadvantage. But in the short run any increase in imports or change in the pattern of imports can and typically does cause at least temporary unemployment in the import-competing lines of production, and any rise in exports increases employment in export lines. The two may not offset in the short run. Protectionism may therefore increase employment in some lines temporarily but not change total employment in the economy in the long run. What is sometimes not explicit in the textbooks is that some of the propositions about trade's effects do depend upon the willingness and ability of a country to restore and maintain full employment in not too long a run if economic forces do not do so automatically. It may or may not be more obvious that a rise in a nation's protectionism to gain at least a temporary advantage in employment in import-competing lines may be offset by foreign retaliatory protectionism that reduces employment in our export lines where we need it more.

Sometimes the textbooks show that there are circumstances in which a country might gain by tariffs to improve the terms of trade of a country. They seldom go so far as to examine the ethics, or even the consequences, of likely retaliation, if done by a wealthy and powerful country like the United States in order to get a bigger share of the gains of trade at the expense of poorer and weaker peoples. Conclusions drawn from the pure theory alone are a poor guide to policy.

Indeed economics does not lead one to question whether there are any reasons to limit the degree of specialization that market forces might bring about for a country, an area, or an individual. Is it healthy for a country to be a "banana republic," its economy and hence the livelihood of its people vitally dependent upon any one export? We know from experience that a one-industry town is not in an ideal economic situation. In the picture *Modern Times,* Charlie Chaplin portrayed a worker reduced to being an inhuman machine tightening a bolt on an assembly line. There is such a thing as too much specialization for a human being. What about for a small area? The old complaint again is that economics needs to pay more attention to all values relevant to a situation, and it typically fails to do so. International economic relations are not reducible to the advantages of relying on comparative advantage alone.

Foreign investment issues tend to be examined much too little. Much of the international trade as well as foreign investment is carried on now by multinational corporations. Some of their operations raise various objections in both home countries and host countries, and these are not dealt with by talking about rationalizing the word "economy" and getting around short-sighted protectionism. Attention should be focused upon the question of what, if anything, can be done by nations or by international controls to reduce or remove grounds for legitimate objections without destroying the advantages of MNCs to both host and home countries. It is only a start to show, as the textbooks tend to do, that if foreign owners receive only the marginal productivity of their foreign investments, rather than what might well be called exploitative rates of return, both the capital-receiving country and the capital-exporting country could gain. Exploitation is not unknown.

The relation between the trade balance and the debtor-creditor position of a country may not be pointed out in some textbooks. The mercantilist notion that an export surplus is desirable (let alone possible for all countries) is usually exploded, as it needs to be, because this idea, which ought to be dead, is still walking around the country and even in the halls of Congress. Sending more goods out of the country than one brings in obviously does not raise the standard of living. Indeed it is possible to do so permanently only by lending others the money to buy the export surplus, and then not collecting on the loan.

Textbooks contend that there is no reason for trade to balance between any two countries even if the total trade of a country should balance. What the books need to add is that the trade balance itself is dependent upon foreign investment situation. In the early history of this country, economic development was aided, as it is for third world countries today, by attracting, that is, borrowing, foreign capital and using it to import goods for development purposes. The result is an import surplus. A country making foreign investments, a capital exporter, has thereby in effect financed a surplus of exports of its goods and services. The former is called a growing debtor country and the latter a growing creditor country. The United States was a growing debtor country until World War I and a growing creditor country thereafter until recently, the switch to a net debtor position coming about the middle of the Reagan administration. A mature creditor nation, no longer lending to others, could enjoy an import surplus and thereby a higher standard of living (if it maintained full employment) by virtue of receiving returns on its prior investments. A country with an accumulated foreign debt, which ceased foreign borrowing, would be obliged to continue to service the debt or reduce it, and this would give it an export surplus, lowering its standard of living at the time as it would consume less than it was producing in order to pay on the debt.

The rate of foreign investment can increase more rapidly, however, than the balance of trade can adjust, and this causes a disequilibrium in the balance of payments at fixed exchange rates. The implication is that under fixed-exchange-rate international monetary systems such as the gold standard or the Bretton Woods System, there can be times when an increasing rate of foreign investment is incompatible with the fixed exchange rates, and either exchange rates must be changed or restraints put upon the rate of foreign investment until exports and returns on the foreign investment catch up. The United States faced this choice in the 1960s but the controversy at the time showed business demanding what was at the time incompatible: both fixed rates for their benefit, and no interference with freedom to invest abroad regardless of balance-of-payments results. Such an issue may arise in the future, so the history needs to be understood.

On a still broader level, there needs to be more adequate treatment of the relation of international economic relations to war or peace. Others besides Marxist-Leninists have pictured war as arising, some say inevitably, from international economic relations. The case can be made that one of the sources of friction between nations historically has lain in their international economic relations. But it is not correct that capitalism requires war, nor that noncapitalist countries could not have economic conflict between them. There is nothing about international economic relations that necessarily leads to war. The fact is that war destroys at great cost the economic gains from peaceful trade and investment relations among nations. Even preparation for war and power politics alignments distort potential mutually beneficial economic relations among nations. It is doubtful whether war has ever produced a net economic benefit for a people, or has been relatively cost-effective. Of course it is only the survivors who are able to evaluate that. In the period of colonialism, present peace-loving nations put many of their international economic relations in a framework created by military aggression and subsequent political control. It is clear that some individuals and businesses gained from colonialism. Colonialism now has a bad name, and it is not clear whether the mother countries benefited on net balance or not, or whether they could have gained more through development of a different type of international economic relations such as now obtain among the industrial powers themselves. MDC-LDC relations are still troublesome, partly because of the heritage from colonialism.

Idealists, of whom we generally need more when realists have made a mess of things, have sometimes taken the position that international economic relations, instead of causing war, can be a major cure for, or rather, preventive of war. After the Hawley-Smoot tariff hike in the Great Depression worsened both international relations and the depression, Cordell Hull in the Franklin Roosevelt administration led the switch to a more liberal foreign trade regime. He argued that the route to both world peace and prosperity lay in expanding international trade and developing an integrated world economy. However, it is naive to suppose that increasing the degree of international economic integration can alone neutralize the inherent instability in a system where each country seeks national security by developing stronger offensive national military capabilities and the other ingredients of the power politics game.

The future may, however, be unlike the past in terms of potential international conflicts over shortages of some of the world's natural resources. It is already apparent that major industrial powers are heavily dependent upon oil, and that they are concerned about access, on favorable terms, to Middle Eastern oil. It is easy to argue for maintaining ready access for all nations to any of the increasingly scarce natural resources, scattered unevenly over the globe as they are.

But that would permit the rich to buy up control in some cases, whereas many of the people of the nation thus selling their resources might want to keep them for their own further development. If they then try to do so and assert their own control over resources within their borders, will outside nations accommodate or will denied access result in war to enable the powerful to get political control of areas and ensure their own exclusive access to some resources? Economists are not talking about the real world if the scope of their analysis is restricted to the theory of comparative advantage and the old arguments against tariffs. What sort of framework for future international economic relations would make most sense and how might it be forged? This is the subject to be wrestled with.

It does not help to have politicians talking as though the issue was simply free trade. Trade always has been and necessarily is managed by government or negotiated between or among governments. That nations have often favored special interests rather than the general interest is easily demonstrated. But, in the nature of the case, there cannot be any demonstration that completely free trade is always in the best interest of every nation with all relevant values taken into account. It is high time for textbooks to deal with trade issues realistically, using all relevant values instead of being restricted to abstract economic theory as though the latter gave sufficient answers to the politico-economic questions.

Some recent developments in the international scene open new opportunities and others are quite problematical. The collapse of Soviet and Eastern European communism has opened new opportunities for international economic relations unclouded by the cold war. Yet the transition to whatever changed economic systems is fraught with many problems that are not being handled well either internally or by outsiders.

The small response of industrialized countries to repeated demands by the less developed countries for a New International Economic Order has been followed by the former countries' touting a new global economy, the most obvious beneficiaries of which seem to be the transnational or multinational corporations. They are the primary globalizers of the world economy. GATT has been succeeded by a new World Trade Organization, which might have been structured better as a forum to deal well with the whole range of politico-economic issues arising internationally, but which seems on the face of it to establish procedures that rule out any effective considerations except whether free trade is hampered. Some reconsideration of its operation will almost certainly be necessary.

Nations have yet to figure out how to take advantage of comparative advantage when they want to do so and how to do so on what might be called a relatively "level playing field." While exchange rates can adjust to differences among countries' price and wage levels, they do not take into account the multitudinous differences in other labor standards or in very different environmental provisions among countries. Leadership by any country in such matters should not be rendered impossible by such things as Dolphin Case. In that case, GATT essentially denied the United States the right to restrict imports of fish from countries whose fishers used fish nets that also trapped dolphins that did not survive. The trade restriction was the only effective way for the United States to influence other countries to take precautions to preserve the dolphin population.

Free trade is a new political mantra serving special interests, for no country is going to stop managing trade and indeed all international economic relations for various purposes, even if it takes time to tame the new WTO. The question is only how intelligently countries manage. Do they merely cave in to all protectionist interests, or do they slowly work out level playing fields that enable each nation to gain without compromising other common interests in each nation? Any trade expansion hurts import-competing sectors of an economy while it may be benefiting the economy as a whole. Trade adjustment assistance is the only proper way to deal with the injury, even though our record with such assistance should be better than it has been. It makes sense to slow down the rate at which adjustment is required, while at the same time trying to speed up the rate at which adjustment is made. As for the economic relations between industrialized and less developed nations, many problems remain. It is not a question of whether on net balance transnational corporations do more good or more harm. The question is whether the alleged harm can be eliminated while the good can be developed. It is almost certainly true that economic development of the less developed countries can be furthered by proper and yet profitable behavior of the transnationals. Yet deals among leaders may not really promote development. There was merit in UNCTAD fears that foreign money might control their economies too much. It is a perennial issue: When money is power, how is it to be controlled in the general interest? Let textbooks and instructors wrestle with such real issues instead of confining themselves merely to the principle of comparative advantage. Then students are better prepared to be citizens.

33. The International Monetary System

The economics textbooks generally explain how the gold standard worked in its heyday. What they do not explain adequately is that it broke down in the interwar period due to a combination of abnormal strains upon it and factors that made those strains too difficult to handle. Relatively small and slow changes were easy to handle, but not the major readjustments in the international economy resulting from the war, including the dead-weight reparations payments and inter-Allied war debts. Great Britain's overvalued pound was also critical. The U.S. gold policies were apparently based on fallacious commodity-theory reasoning as part of a set of depression recovery policies. International monetary relations in the 1930s were somewhat chaotic. During the subsequent war, negotiators wanted to avoid a return to that chaos, and that led to the establishment of the Bretton Woods System. This in turn broke down as the fixed dollar became untenable by the early 1970s, primarily as a result of the increasing competitiveness of Europe and Japan after they recovered from war and forged ahead, while exchange rates did not adjust to these changes. Both experiences show that the advantages of a stable rate system depend upon sufficient short-run liquidity, an adequate adjustment mechanism, and the necessity of adjusting rates when economic change alters what would be equilibrium rates. The alternative of exchange rates fluctuating freely with demand and supply has advantages and disadvantages also.

The question as to what determines equilibrium rates is sometimes answered by the purchasing-power parity theory, the theory that the relative purchasing powers of currencies determines their exchange rates at equilibrium. The theory is plausible, appealing, and sometimes appears to explain changes in rates. Clearly domestic inflation in a country tends to raise the prices of foreign currencies also, as it increases demand for them relative to supply, since inflation penalizes the country's exports and makes imports more competitive. But the theory that movements in exchange rates, measuring changes in the external value of a currency, must move proportionately to changes in domestic price levels, measuring changes in the internal value of a currency, is erroneous for reasons not usually pointed out. Compare the composition of two index numbers, a domestic price index and an index of exchange rates. The domestic price index contains prices of many domestic goods and services that do not enter into international trade and so do not enter into the exchange-rate index computation, and these prices do not necessarily change to the same degree as the prices that enter the latter index. International capital movements may at times have a major direct effect on exchange rates, but these specific flows do not directly enter the computation of the domestic price index, so they may also cause the movements in the two indexes to diverge.

A country's exchange rates are now often said to be overvalued or undervalued. Essentially that means out of line with what would produce something like equilibrium in the country's total balance of payments. The consequence of overvaluation is to make imports artificially cheap and the country's exports artificially expensive to foreign buyers. Undervaluation, by contrast, gives an artificial advantage to exports and makes imports artificially expensive. If a currency has been pegged at an artificially high level by a country, it will draw down the country's foreign exchange reserves and will likely sooner or later force devaluation of the currency. If pegged at an artificially low level, it can be maintained only so long as other countries' banks are willing to continue buying more of the artificially pegged currency than they can sell, or if the country finances its export surplus by lending others the money to buy the excess exports. If exchange rates are free to fluctuate instead of being pegged, it would seem as though the market rate would always be at least a short-run equilibrium rate and the terms "overvalued" and "undervalued" would be misnomers. But the terms continue to be used to suggest that the market rates are reflecting other forces that are distorting the trade balance or current account balance in ways that those using the terms consider undesirable.

In a system of freely fluctuating rates, the rates can be quite volatile in the short run, sometimes aggravated by speculation, and this introduces additional hazards for international business transactions. So nations often try to "manage" their exchange rates to a limited extent. If the nations on the other end of an exchange rate help to stabilize them, or at least not hinder, and if the countries try merely to reduce erratic fluctuations around an equilibrium rate rather than try to stabilize at other than an equilibrium rate, the efforts may be fairly successful. However, a major factor upsetting stability in the rates and in current account balances of nations can arise from nations' conducting independent macroeconomic policies that in a sense don't match. Efforts to coordinate national macroeconomic policies are still in their infancy, but high-level discussions of the problems involved in doing so or failing to do so are now quite common. Unfortunately the press often uses the term "dirty float" for any interference by government in exchange markets, not distinguishing between efforts to reduce erratic instability and efforts to get an unfair advantage for exports.

Not enough attention is paid in the textbooks to significance of changes in world capital markets. The fact is that short-term and long-term capital markets are now international. And the magnitude of the flows in those markets totally dwarfs the trade flows. Indeed there is now an enormous amount of speculation on movements of exchange rates included in the short-term capital flows. The result of this is that exchange rates are dominated by the financial flows rather than by comparative advantage. This is very significant. The competitiveness of a nation's industries is now less the determinant of its international trade position than is the money sloshing around in the world's financial markets. That sloshing around is affected by relative interest rates, themselves affected by national macroeconomic policies, by expectations as to short-run movements in prices of financial assets in securities exchanges, and so on. Unemployment in import-competing and export industries is thus hostage to unrelated financial manipulations by nationals in one's own and other countries. This is an unintended and disturbing result of the development of the world's financial markets, including the foreign exchange markets.

It should not be blindly assumed that this does not create a real problem, or that it will work out well automatically. At present unilateral efforts to deal with the problem are unlikely to be very successful in providing satisfactory solutions. The IMF is not presently set up to deal with the problem. It is not clear either what global regulations would even be possible, let alone successful, even if the framework for them existed, which it does not as yet. In its absence, economic nationalisms will likely produce efforts to deal with the problem unilaterally. Nobel Prize winner James Tobin has made one interesting proposal, however: that a tax be placed on exchange-rate transactions high enough to knock out the speculators but not so high as to hinder significantly the trade or long-term capital flows.

The Future Development
of Economic Systems

34. The Economic Roles of Government

The economic roles of government have obviously differed between different types of economic systems. Even within a given system debate often rages over its proper economic roles.

Economics used to be called political economy. Economists and others who use economics typically use it to argue for or against certain governmental economic policies which are determined by a political process. Some policies are aimed at what are considered to be economic problems, as one of the few ways the public can deal with problems. In modern industrial economies, government roles are necessarily more important than in a primitive rural economy.

A democratic political process is presumed to operate in the public interest as distinct from private interests which may not always be identical with that. It is clear that the process often fails to serve the public interest as well as it does some specific private interests that are well organized. So legislation and administration are sometimes unduly influenced by the latter, as the electoral process itself may be. For the government's economic roles to actually work in the public interest is not only a matter of knowing what policies that would require, but of actually making the democratic political process work as it should. That is a responsibility of the general public and the ethics of political personages. More important is whether the system is set up to weight informed citizenry more than monied interests.

Any discussion of government roles needs to start by making the distinction between the government sector of the economy and the government's relation to the other sectors of the economy. Any economy other than one of pure anarchism, if such be possible, has a government sector of the economy, and at the other end of a spectrum presumably the entire economy would be in the government sector. There is no example of either that is quite that extreme. People legitimately differ as to what should and should not be in the government sector, and what is in fact included in any country has changed through history. People often fail to distinguish between the historical changes in the size of the government sector of the economy and changes in the scope of that sector, typically thinking bigger government represents an expansion of its scope at the expense of the private sector of the economy, although often that is not the case. Much of the increase in the level of federal government spending in the United States in the twentieth century is an increase in military expenditures, most of which are purchases from businesses. The increase does not represent government's undertaking a new type of production instead of leaving it in the hands of the private sector. The large increase in federal government transfer payments is what the term implies, a purchasing power transfer, not an instance of moving production of something from the private sector to the government sector of the economy.

The reason for emphasizing the point, as some textbooks do not, is that failure to make the distinction between size and scope of the government sector leads to charges that the growth of the federal government indicates "creeping socialism," which worries some people. Much steam would be taken out of this charge if one could identify the portion of government expenditures at each level of government that is government production replacing what had been private production.

The growth of government expenditures at the state and local levels, which is also substantial, is explained largely by population growth, increased numbers of automobiles, and desires for better transportation and better schooling as people's incomes rise. None of this represents an extension of the scope of the government sector after the establishment of public education.

Obviously the economic role of government now includes a large public school system, extending from elementary through university levels. This provides the private business sector of the economy a level of basic training for their employees that is essential for business but that individual businesses simply could not afford to finance for employees who cannot be tied to the individual firm. So not everything in the government sector of the economy can properly be regarded as being at the expense of private enterprise, as some ideology would have one think. Indeed in education, private schools operate along with the public schools at all levels, so even in this field, public does not spell the end of private.

Changes in the scope of the public sector in the United States have been smaller than changes in the size of that sector, although some changes, often controversial, have occurred. Urban private streetcar systems have largely given way to public bus systems, as one example of such change, a change related to the unprofitability of the private systems. In the Reagan administration, privatization was an effort to move things from the public to the private sector.

The government sector might also be thought of as including what can be called collective consumption (as distinct from government production)—such things as tax-supported parks, and even roads, some built by the private sector. The concept of public goods now appears in the textbooks as an indication of why some things are in the public sector at least in one sense. But it must be noted that while military defense is considered a public good, most military goods production is in the private sector, as noted.

The efficiency of the government sector of the economy is of major concern because government is not under competitive market pressures to be efficient, and some people are always succumbing to the ever-present temptations to pad expenses for someone's benefit, as well as other forms of corruption. The textbooks seldom talk about who and what businesses do the corrupting of government people.

The decision-making process in government should be guided by the cost-benefit principle, but even where economic benefits for someone or some group do not distort the process, it is often impossible to make an unarguable case for the cost and benefit estimates. Benefits are often nonmonetary and hard or impossible to reduce to monetary equivalents.

To turn now to the relation of government to the private sectors of the economy, there is danger that students may gloss over the story that government provides the legal framework within which the market processes operate. It must be heavily stressed that this is the most important and basic economic role of government in relation to the private sectors of the economy. Historically such a necessary framework for markets grew out of customs and understandings sometimes enforced by "courts" established by traders. The framework now consists of such important things as contract law, property law, and so on. Then there is the legislation that established the corporate form of business organization, a social invention with such benefits that corporations have come to dominate the business world. The valuable privileges granted the corporate form of business organization by law include limited liability of the stockholder owners, and bankruptcy provisions that enable corporations to start over in some circumstances by inflicting losses on their creditors. One reason for paying close attention to the fact that corporations are a valuable but especially privileged creation of society is to put in perspective the frequent complaint of corporate executives that government has no right to interfere or regulate the conduct of incorporated businesses.

If the invisible hand made famous by Adam Smith's followers sufficed to make the market always work as well as the concept suggests, government economic roles would be less than in fact they are. Government is sometimes said to be needed as a policeman of the marketplace, maintaining free contract so it will actually produce mutual benefits. Frank Knight, the conservative economist who was the initial intellectual leader of the Chicago school of economics, used to stress the fact that the condition for free contract to be mutually beneficial was the absence of force and fraud. If both sides to an economic transaction know what they are doing and are not forced to make a bad deal, each side will enter a transaction only if it will gain by doing so. In fact, government's role as policeman of the market necessarily gives only limited help to reduce force and fraud in economic transactions.

Clearly, competition, not perfect competition but competition, is a major factor in both Adam Smith's invisible-hand argument and in actuality as inducing markets to serve consumers better than otherwise. But competition is not always self-maintaining, hence government antitrust policies. One role of government is to help maintain or restore competition in the interest of consumers, and more than incidentally in the interest of business competitors, or would-be competitors, to be free from unfair monopolistic attacks upon them. Somewhat the opposite sometimes happens, namely sometimes government is utilized by special-interest groups to place artificial restraints upon competition for the economic advantage of the special interest. This is ordinarily to be regarded as an instance where democracy is not working well to serve and protect the public interest, and where that interest is being subverted.

Sometimes government places limits upon the terms of contracts, as when it sets price floors (e.g., minimum wage laws) or ceilings (e.g., rent control laws), or government may regulate prices as in public utility rate regulation, or may sometimes freeze prices to combat inflation.

Early in the Industrial Revolution in England, factory reform legislation was passed to protect the safety of workers and to limit the hours of work. Students would find it very instructive to read the arguments made at the time against such measures. Some spoke of the alleged rights of business to do as it pleased without interference, and some about the prospective destruction of business profitability. These are among the arguments that continue to be heard every time there is any new public interest legislation proposed. Laissez-faire talk is not heard, however, when business calls on government to help promote some business interests. In any case, we do not hear anymore, as we did in the early nineteenth century, from both Christian ministers and economists, that there must be no interference with the God-given freedom of women and children to work more than twelve hours a day in the mills. Besides, it was argued, all the profits are made in the last hours of the day, so cutting them off would destroy all profits and hence wreck the capitalist economic system. It turned out not to be true; indeed productivity went up with a reduction in hours of work required. There has been some ethical progress in the legal framework in which the private sector of the economy operates profitably.

The more general problem is that private marginal cost and social marginal cost are not always identical. The market is governed by the former, and public policy needs to be governed by the latter. The instances now discussed in the economics textbooks are referred to as externalities. It is sometimes easier to describe them than to conceive generally acceptable policies that could get private and social costs to coincide. More attention will almost certainly have to be paid in the future to how the government can induce the economy to operate on a sustainable basis, which it does not do as yet. It is now overloading its life support system not only by pollution but in wide areas by over-cropping, overgrazing, overfishing, and overforesting and thus depleting the natural resource base on whose potential the economy rests.

Some public policy toward international economic relations is unavoidable, so here is another inescapable economic role for government. A wide range of possibilities exists here, and what we had to say in that connection has already been said.

Since the Great Depression of the 1930s, national governments in industrial economies have undertaken a positive macroeconomic policy role to reduce economic instability, unemployment, and inflation, and to promote growth and balance-of-payments equilibrium, despite those who continue to argue that it can only make matters worse. For much longer it has been an economic role of government to exercise some control over money, for the experience of its failure to exercise proper control was very unfortunate. Indeed some failure in that respect received a lot of attention in connection with the debacle in the savings and loan industry. A sound money and financial system is so important to the whole economy that this type of government regulation has raised less controversy than some of the other economic roles of government, although currently new financial developments are again little regulated.

Finally, government in its taxing and spending policies inevitably has some effect on the distribution of income and wealth, and there is continuous pressure on government from various sides to rig these policies deliberately so as to have an affect in one direction or another on the distribution. In one of its economic roles, then, government affects the distribution inadvertently or deliberately. Throughout history, it should be noted, government has taxed lower-income people to support a well-to-do elite. The progressive income tax is a historically unique social invention. But students should be aware that this does not result in income's being redistributed downward to any very significant extent. That it is not redistributed is not due only to the so-called loopholes, some of which are always available to those with high incomes, but to the regressivity of much of the tax structure. Also, the biggest part of the transfer payments system goes from middle class to middle class, despite the public impression that most goes to welfare mothers or other poor. An examination of distribution data shows a rather consistent fraction of income for each quintile in the income distribution, the high degree of inequality holding fairly steady until recently when inequality increased considerably. Government may now be redistributing up, but at least it is not obviously redistributing down enough to check rising inequality, or, prior to recent years, to significantly change high and fairly stable inequality. Certainly there is a case for government's limiting the degree of inequality when it gets as great as it now is in this country. CEO pay levels have reached ridiculous levels at a time while we still have poverty and a large number of working poor. Progressive income taxes should be strengthened, not weakened, and the inheritance tax strengthened, to reduce excessive inequality if business will not itself reduce it.

Recently the so-called new right has resurrected a blatant attack on the economic roles of government. It argues that capitalism is an economic system that has improved living standards immensely and increased people's economic freedom and must not be interfered with by government. To be sure, living standards have been immensely increased, but it has not been an uninterfered-with economic freedom for business that has accomplished that. Beginning with the factory reform legislation in the 1820s, there has been a long line of legislative restrictions on business, beginning with not being allowed to hire women and children twelve hours a day.

It is not really true, though it sounds good, that that government is best that governs least. That was a slogan that may have made sense when government was less needed because the economy was largely rural. But in today's economy the problem is not that government power is feared by the average citizen, but that private economic power is so great, and the average citizen cannot protect himself against it, that some protection can be furnished only by government. How else can the consumer be protected against meat packers selling meat containing bacteria that will make him sick, except by adequate government regulations and inspection? Can labor protect itself sufficiently against unsafe working conditions? Have residential areas no right to use government zoning regulations to protect themselves against commercial or industrial developments in their midst? The new right either puts too much faith in the saintliness of business by its belief that no regulations are needed, or it doesn't care about the results if there are none. Labor unions can no longer get a fair break in bargaining; if management claims an impasse, it can enforce its last offer, and if labor strikes, nonunion labor can be hired permanently.

To be sure, bureaucrats have sometimes gone overboard with stupid regulations, but the cure is to be found case by case, not by a cry to get government off our (business's) backs so business can do anything it pleases. Getting government off our (the public's) backs is largely a matter of reducing taxes, and that can be done, and the deficit ended very simply by reducing our still bloated military expenditures; but that is not desired because that would cut the very profitable business of the military-industrial complex. Indeed much government expenditure is a matter of purchases from business, even apart from the military. Money doesn't just go to government, it goes through government to business and people, so the only question is whether the transfers are warranted, case by case. In many cases (the pork barrel) they are not, but are the result of special-interest pressures and politicians granting each other's wishes.

It is a very real question as to whether government can be run more efficiently, given elected officials' penchant for using their office to appoint friends and relatives to other positions or being corrupted by special-interest pressures. Waste and the pork barrel are still in evidence in both political parties. In connection with the latter, why do we put all the blame on the government officials and none on the business interests that do the corrupting? The standards of honesty in government are clearly higher here than in many countries, but still have a way to go. The real problem of our nominally democratic government is a political and electoral system that permits those with lots of money, including special business interests, to outbuy others, especially for the publicity that seems to control election to public office. The Supreme Court does not yet recognize that this is corruption of the democratic political process, not a simple free speech issue.

There is a dishonest way to go in reducing government, and that is to propose merely returning each function to the several states. It is surprising that business would want this, inasmuch as businesses usually do not want to have to adjust to fifty different state laws. However, the fact is that each state legislature is easily played off against its neighboring states, told that it cannot have legislation more restrictive than its neighboring states, or taxes higher than the neighboring states. This does not prevent all differences, but it keeps the differences small. Really effective legislation in many cases must be at the federal level, for the states can easily be prevented from "getting out of line."

Then there is our safety net, including social security. The Reagan administration cut people off the disability rolls without legally required hearings, and when the courts required adherence to the laws, a cabinet-level government official said they would think about whether to comply. This from a government that called itself conservative, and while Reagan announced he was protecting the safety net.

Without taking a thing from private insurance, which is a wonderful way of generalizing the willingness of farmers to join to rebuild the farmer's barn that burned down, there are some things that social insurance can do that private insurance cannot do. We have yet to devise a universal health insurance scheme and add it to our social security system. Until we do, there will be more and more people without medical insurance or adequate medical insurance.

National security has always been considered the first responsibility of government, though it is mentioned last here. It is so noncontroversial that we have been scared into levels of military spending that make no sense. During the cold war aimed at the Soviet Union, we became able to destroy every militarily significant Soviet target from two submarines (Carter said one), yet we stockpiled thousands of nuclear bombs many times as powerful as those that destroyed Hiroshima and Nagasaki. There was room to debate whether, if a hot war had started, and the United States and the Soviet Union had used all their nukes, the human race would have survived; certainly modern civilization would not have survived. And we stockpiled these nukes in the name of realism and national security! Such idiocy is hard to explain. Textbooks should not gloss over it with the platitude that national security is a major function of government. It is indeed, but modern military technology can destroy any country halfway around the world, and that has made military establishments as obsolete as castles for national security. It will be possible for national security to be restored only when all national military establishments are reduced to levels needed for internal policing, so no nation can threaten another, and adequate nonviolent means are required and available to settle international disputes. Law and government are needed now at the international level as well as the national and local levels. World federalists have been arguing that strongly since the end of World War II. It is time that nations wake up to see what is required of them for national security. They can gain their own security only by giving up the right and the power to destroy other nations. No one in his right mind wants wars anymore, but we fail to consider how to end them. War doesn't arise from the belligerence of human nature; it requires a draft and propaganda to get strangers to maim and kill each other. Nothing compares with war in the unnecessary human suffering caused; nothing would enhance human well-being, and in economic terms utility, so much as ending wars. Let the market stop driving military production, and international wars can stop. Every state now depends upon military production to a greater or lesser extent. This was deliberate, and it makes it possible for the military to "blackmail" senators who would cut the military budget very much. It is time students are helped to face the real issues of national security. And if people want to get government off their backs, where better than to cut the burden of over $260 billion going unnecessarily to the military? The peacetime cost of the military, year after year, increases rather than reduces national insecurity, yet we keep paying because the public cannot think of any alternative. It is time to conceive that a very limited government at the world level is needed to keep law and order between the leaders of nations, at a fraction of the cost of preparing for the horrors of war, war that political leaders can otherwise foment.

"To concede the virtues of the market is not to embrace laissez-faire. A market system, however inventive, is not self-regulating. It does not add up to a socially defensible allocation of either private income or public investment. . . . Markets often punish innocent bystanders and reward unproductive speculators. Market values tend to crowd out social values. . . . The real debate is about how to structure the departures from pure laissez-faire, not whether to have them."[23]

It is high time that we get off the antigovernment kick and get government to operate properly in the public interest. That will require politicians to quit promising what they can't deliver, and the public to go to the polls and vote their own real interest, including government regulation of business, reduced inequality, and universal health insurance.

Government clearly has not been representing the general public interest as well as it should in a democracy. It is not in general true that what is good for General Motors is good for the country, though it is in general true that what is good for the country is good for General Motors. Business interests and the interests of well-to-do investors are often better served by government than is the public. Why the public does not see this, go to the polls, and vote their own interest is a good question. Dropping out and not voting is not going to cure the government's failure to promote the general interest better. Most people are employees, not employers and big investors, so it is employees' interests that more largely determine the public interest where there is a conflict, although clearly employees and employers have a common interest in the health of the economy, and that requires less inequality.

The political process, aided by the mass communications media, needs to seek to develop a broader consensus on what is really in the public interest, rather than doing everything it can to create greater divisiveness. Whatever it will take to improve the political process is very important indeed. That should indeed be our common cause. Textbooks should call for that.

35. Comparative Economic Systems

Unexpected economic system changes initiated in the late 1980s quickly outdated the defective standard textbook treatments of comparative economic systems. How textbooks should now handle the subject receives some comments here.

The future of communist and former communist-controlled systems is unclear and will likely remain so for some time. It is obvious that turmoil is associated with their breakdown. Many people, some economists, are oversimplifying the problems of transition to our type of economy. It is uncertain how many people or leaders in ex-communist countries want to copy us or know where they want to go. It may be that most care primarily for protecting and improving their standard of living even in the transition. But, if in the transitions their standards of living go down instead of improving, as expected, many ex-communist countries may again resort to authoritarian controls, at least for a time.

Whatever the outcome, the basic practical and ideological issues that should be considered in the study of comparative economic systems have not disappeared as a result of the big changes in the former USSR and Eastern Europe.

Perhaps there will be a lesser tendency now to take a bipolarized view of the world, every country called either capitalist or socialist-communist. What students should learn from their textbook first is that each country is to some extent unique in culture and economy, and the differences among countries typically classified as having a common type of economic system sometimes have been as great as those between some pairs in different systems. The differences between industrialized and less developed countries are usually greater than between capitalist and communist industrial countries in significant respects.

Economies differ in degree in many respects, so simple bipolar classifications misrepresent in oversimplifying. Defining "pure" capitalism or another "pure" system posits figments of the imagination.

Ideologies exaggerate the real differences, but it is still useful for us to understand what grounds, if any, there are for the standard criticisms of capitalism and its ideology by socialists and of socialism by its critics. Marxism as an ideology needs to be understood and distinguished from so-called Marxist economies.

All actual economies are quite complex mixtures of common elements. The differences in mix, role, and degree pertain to such things as government roles, the nature and roles of markets, and the patterns, privileges, and roles of property ownership. And all these factors have changed over time in countries of each "type."

The market versus nonmarket economy distinction is sometimes drawn too sharply. Markets are employed in all economies, and textbooks should emphasize that, then show the differences among them in illustrative countries. Centrally controlled economies typically have, and have had, consumer goods markets (but not the degree of consumer sovereignty that exists in our country) and labor markets (controlled to some extent, though not usually to the degree often alleged).

In no country is resource allocation controlled completely by consumer sovereignty in markets. Galbraith puts a different light on the matter with his extreme picture of our own economy as one where consumers are caged squirrels who are kept running and turning the wheels of business while seeking the bait business provides, rather than being sovereign consumers whom business serves slavishly. This picture exaggerates but perhaps not a lot more than does consumer sovereignty.

Every economy has a government sector that allocates a substantial share of economic resources. In a democratic political system, the public presumably has ultimate control over such resource allocation, but it is through a political process, not through the market. In the heat of debate over socialist tendencies, the general rise in government expenditures in some countries has been alleged to be a slide toward socialism, meaning a growth of government at the expense of private business. As suggested in the essay on government in this book, that usually misrepresents the situation, for the added money spent by government is usually not to pay government employees to produce something previously produced by a private business, but to buy something more produced by private business. Our huge military expenditures support directly and indirectly a very large group of private business firms producing military goods, as everyone knows. So allocation of resources through government is not necessarily at the expense of private enterprise, though it is a very different thing for business to be dependent upon market competition and to be primarily dependent upon government contracts.

To be sure, markets, consumers, and private business play a much lesser role in economies dominated by communist party governments. Their centrally controlled economies have worked to the degree that they have, partly because not everything was indeed controlled centrally. Such systems were inefficient, which could be seen easily enough. But the idea that market pricing was an adequate universal guide to efficient resource allocation is accepted uncritically in this section of the textbooks. In fact, we also reject that criterion in some instances, including those of public goods and "externalities," and some other secular and religious ideologies reject the market criterion in principle. It should be recognized that there is room for disagreement over the extent to which market pricing should be the sole guide to resource allocation.

Western European economies are sometimes referred to as welfare states, though the term has no precise accepted meaning. Among the things often referred to in that context, however, is the rejection of the view that markets should be the sole determinants of the distribution of income and wealth, or of the level of employment. "Safety nets" and various forms of "social security" for all individuals have become common and supplement various types of insurance offered by business firms. There is room for debate over the character and extent of such subsystems, debate more rational when ideological labels are not thrown around as if they could be definitive arguments.

The dominant form of business establishment in our country is the corporation, an important institutional invention given designated legal powers and privileges, and hence subject to social regulation, as is all activity in nonanarchist societies. When it comes to the comparative-systems section of the book treatment of private property, it is well to remember what presumably was learned in the section on forms of business enterprise, namely that control and ownership are largely divorced in the modern corporation, and that owners are primarily traders in corporate stock; so much of the Jeffersonian case for private ownership, while not wrong, is inapplicable to the modern corporation.

The separation of political power and economic power is a matter of great importance, as is the limitation of both, as is generally agreed in this country. The textbooks often make less clear the extent to which, even for us, economic power has political power. One need not go overboard in relating them, as do our radicals, in order to become realistic about this or about the extent to which "command" has pertained within our own business system. A little realistic American history is indispensable in textbooks for those who have not worked in firms where the boss was as autocratic in his realm as any dictator, with as little check on arbitrary actions. Such perspective is essential if people are to understand the real issues in economic life and how they have been handled here and elsewhere. The accountability of both political and economic power is a bigger problem in some politico-economic systems than in others, and at different points in their history.

It is of special importance that textbooks, though they often neglect it, emphasize that freedoms be discussed and analyzed in the plural, not treated as though one was just for or against freedom. There are many freedoms from, and freedoms for, that need to be distinguished individually. There is such a thing as legal freedom to monopolize or a legal protection of freedom from monopoly and preservation of freedom to compete. The choices of freedoms in different economies can be compared, a matter not clarified sufficiently by speaking of the free world.

What everybody enjoys most about comparative economic systems is not learning the often dry facts about different economies, but, after generalizing about systems by oversimplifying and misrepresenting much reality, pronouncing summary judgments on others and our own. More important than the necessary job of exposing students to the complex reality is the need, often completely neglected, for the textbook to introduce them to an intellectually respectable evaluation methodology, with special attention to both criteria and attribution. One question is which comparisons are really fair. Countries may be at quite different stages of economic development, so direct standard of living comparisons are not likely fair. In any case there is the problem of attribution. Is every aspect of performance to be attributed to the economic system? Since all else is never the same, this in general will not do. The situation faced by different countries might account for a lot of the difference in how well they do at some given time period. Other than that, the likelihood is that much of the difference in performance is due to differences in technology. If indeed the system makes a significant difference too, and that is what we are most interested in, what aspect of the system can be properly argued or shown to make what difference, and how does it do so, that is, what is the mechanism by which the difference is brought about? And how do we relate that to the fact that the culture and ideology of a people may make quite a difference in how any given set of institutions works and what results they produce? Another simple unarguable fact is that with a given economic system, the outcomes differ a lot with the economic policies followed. Whether a country has high inflation is more a matter of policies followed than of the type of economic system. And policies are partly a matter of leadership and of the way a political process works or is worked by leaders at one time or another.

Obviously the problem in any country is to provide an incentive system that makes private interest and public interest coincide insofar as possible. It is obvious that no country solves that problem perfectly, and while comparisons may be helpful, to be useful one must face the practical problem. That requires focusing attention on how one's own system might be enabled to do better in that regard, not being satisfied with gloating over how badly some other country seems to us to be doing. Remember when thinking about the public interest in high productivity that the market does not measure all social values properly, and GNP is never to be regarded as a measure of economic or social well-being, so a better concept of productivity in terms of social well-being needs to be kept in mind.

The tragic outcome in Yugoslavia should not lead to dismissal of all inquiry into the actual and possible roles of labor in different economies. After all, the vast majority of people are properly classified as labor rather than management. Labor often has had a purely subservient role, but in some countries there are various forms of labor-management cooperation, in others labor unions play weak or strong economic or a political roles, in some firms labor has representation on the board of management, in some firms they own part of the stock, and some failed firms have been taken over by the laborers. Yugoslavia alone tried a total system of worker control. The problems and the merits or demerits of different economic roles for labor are a very important topic that deserves thorough treatment in a comparative systems course.

In discussing individual countries, or even the big continents, which differ in major ways, it is hoped that the textbook pays attention to the matters discussed in this essay and to what might be identified as the special problems of each country, and how easy or difficult it may be for each to make its proper contribution in dealing with the world problems of the twenty-first century: international political and economic relations, war, internal violence, population, environment, democratization and humanization of economies or justice, and quality of life—what ideological, technological, and system changes may be required or helpful, as well as the quality of leadership needed and the appropriateness of various types of policies.

36. Economic Development

Economic development could be treated in the textbook in various ways. It could deal with the historical development of the West out of a feudal system or the economic development of the United States, though both of these are usually left to economic history books. Usually the focus is upon the less developed areas of the world, primarily in Asia, Africa, and Latin America, where about three-fourths of the world population lives. Since World War II and the decline of the colonial system, much attention has been on the question of how, and even whether, these areas and the majority of the human race can escape the poverty trap as have most people in the more industrialized countries. It would certainly seem as though this issue should be considered as vastly more important than most of the other things analyzed in the textbook, or many of the other things with which we concern ourselves. But the question is, how do the things we have learned in other contexts apply to this big problem, and what else is important in this connection. Indeed what, if anything, can any readers of the textbook do about the matter anyway, individually or as citizens with their own votes on government policies.

Economists sometimes construct models of economic development, centering attention on such matters as the saving-investment rate. It is obviously difficult for poor people to save much, so outside capital can at least help some if properly used, as can some forms of public and private aid, especially if these bring in human skills or technology, which is in as short supply as capital in the less developed countries.

The economic problem can be stated as one of raising the per-hour productivity of human labor, so much economics ought to be applicable. The economies of these countries are dominated by subsistence agriculture, with many people subsisting on inadequate diets on farms and in cities. So increasing agricultural productivity is important, and then using newly released or already unemployed labor to produce other things to raise the standards of living. It is fairly easy to say such things, but it is quite another for a people to make all the changes in their way of life and in their social and economic organization that are necessary. To say economic organizational changes are needed is not to say that it is just a matter of countries' adopting capitalist institutions or socialist institutions. Indeed such ideological debate is almost entirely irrelevant and meaningless to such people except as it has been connected by some people to the old colonialism.

What the textbook needs to point out is that the process of economic development is fundamentally a process of cultural and social change on which economics can shed almost no light. If we look at the transformation of Western Europe from a feudal system to modern industrialism, we see that it involves several centuries during which there was a whole series of revolutionary changes. Some of them were economic in nature, including agricultural, commercial, and industrial revolutions. These were accompanied by social revolutions in which the landholding and clerical classes lost their dominance to commercial and business classes. Political revolutions were also involved, first from feudal lords to kings, then from kings to parliaments. Not least important were the ideological revolutions: the Renaissance, the Reformation and counter-Reformation, the period called the Enlightenment, and the scientific revolution. It is important for economic development that economic and other problems be viewed as problems and that at least a semi-scientific approach to them be taken, rather than their being approached with a sort of fatalism that supposes nothing effective can be done or that things are as they have always been and are supposed to be or at least always will be.

Barbara Ward has written in *Rich Nations and Poor Nations* that what we are witnessing in the post–World War II period is the incomplete revolution. The revolutions that destroyed Western feudalism did not occur simultaneously in the somewhat different and varied cultures of Asia, Africa, and Latin America, but some comparable changes are starting to occur, and may be necessary for the sort of economic development to occur that could enable their vast populations to escape the poverty trap. They need improved technologies, though a jump to the most modern technology is not possible or appropriate. Schumacher[24] has written that they need technologies available to everyone for small-scale production, not a jump into capital-intensive mass production. One of their biggest problems is that they start with such large populations, and since World War II their populations have been growing at historically unprecedented rates, especially in terms of absolute numbers if not all in percentage rates. It is thus very difficult for development to outpace population growth, for it takes some investment just to keep the standard of living from falling, and much more to raise the capital-to-population ratio and spread new technology widely to raise the standard of living for more than an elite few. The textbook should not dodge this issue, for it is part of the reality, though we would rather not know it. And there is no scientific basis for assurance that the population growth problem will be self-limiting this time other than through the terrible Malthusian checks.

37. Growth and Sustainable Economies

Textbooks don't usually prepare one for the emphasis on the desirability of growth found in almost any community and often taken as a proper object of national economic policy. It is easy to see why many businesses want growth: It means an enlargement of their markets even if it is only growth of population. That at least keeps sales of diapers first and everything that follows later at a steady or rising level. If in addition there is growth in per-capita income, sales of almost everything increases further. It creates jobs and it keeps tax receipts rising for governments. If the rise is in per-capita incomes, it makes it possible for real incomes of many to rise, and hence mutes possible conflict over income distribution.

But there are sometimes undesired effects of growth beyond certain points. Urban and suburban areas become crowded, traffic problems worsen, and the amount of time wasted commuting grows. These and other very real economic costs that are not measured by our standard economic measures also decrease the quality of life.

And when growth is viewed on a world scale, it should be apparent that it is not a desirable or even a possible long-run objective on a finite planet. It has been only a few decades when there has been much public recognition of the implications of continued population growth and economic growth on the environment. Environment needs to be regarded as providing not only our economic base in its natural resource capital but even our very life support system. Now we talk about the problems of pollution and depletion as problems that must be faced, since the human race has expanded to the point where it has very significant environmental effects at a macro level and not only in some local areas.

Pollution becomes a problem when the absorptive capacity of the environment is exceeded by pollutants that threaten to alter the environmental balance in ways harmful to humans. Unfortunately we often do not have complete proof of how harmful something will be until too late, so some people refuse to take sufficient preventive measures and instead gamble other people's futures. Posterity cannot vote currently. Both prevention and cleanup of pollution are costly, so often resisted without realizing that the costs of doing nothing might in the end be much higher. Some decline in productivity appears attributable to antipollution efforts because the productivity measure includes the costs but not the unmeasured and often less measurable benefits. One cost that is sometimes obvious is job loss in some lines created by antipollution programs. What might not be recognized is that the money costs of the programs are largely direct or indirect labor costs, so in general antipollution efforts are job-creating more than job-destroying.

Textbooks typically argue that direct regulations or prohibitions of certain pollution is bad, and that it is always adequate and best to tax pollution, thus using the price system to internalize what had been an external cost. The economist's bias has some merit, but the issue should not be closed so dogmatically and without reference to how much ability producers may have in some cases to pass on the tax with minimal effect in reducing pollution. The amount of pressure it takes to change behavior varies. Politicians are unwilling to exert much pressure to reduce chlorofluorocarbons (CFC) production and use lest it have adverse economic effects on some businesses. The public did not know for a long time that a majority of the CFC use was in the military-industrial complex where there could have been complete control of how much effort was made to eliminate their use. So extensive use continues, whatever the effect on the globe's ozone layer may turn out to be. Why do textbooks pussyfoot on such issues?

As for depletion, it is still easy to ignore the limits to growth on a finite planet. But an economy that is geared to extensive and growing use of virgin raw materials is not indefinitely sustainable on that basis. It should be obvious that eventually recycling materials will necessarily become the rule wherever possible, not just a small marginal effort. Costs will necessarily rise as resources become more scarce and as more must be recycled, and technological advances will be necessary to reduce the adverse impact on standards of living.

The energy problem has already received attention, with some research showing that there are still large potentials for conservation in energy use through such things as energy-efficient housing, mass transit, and video-conferencing to reduce travel. The oil age will end, despite the economics that shows why the search for reserves has kept thirty-five years of reserves for some time (get your instructor to tell you also about Hubbert's Hump), and despite economists' assurance that the rise of oil prices will pay to extract more costly oil indefinitely. Here the engineer needs to be heard when he points out that prices do not alone govern, and that the oil age will end when the amount of energy needed to access more oil equals and then exceeds the energy obtainable from it. It does not really require any abstruse analysis to recognize that in the long run, our only safe energy source must be solar, unless some way is found to tap nuclear fusion process heat while containing it without contact with anything. When the half-life of some fission products is 25,000 years, there is likely no way to be sure of the safety of nuclear waste and nuclear plant disposal. Solar energy can be tapped in many ways, including biomass sources, without creating the global heat problem to which all other sources add.

The military turns out to be a major environmental culprit. It gobbles up untold amounts of materials of all sorts, not for direct human benefit, but for the potential that we might destroy all of it in killing each other off. I was taught that the Mesabi range would provide iron ore almost forever, then World War II saw us use up much of it throwing its products at other nations. One fighter plane, after its fuel consumption had been improved, uses more fuel per hour than I use in my car in a year. And for years we maintained many planes aloft all the time lest the Soviets pull something. Expensive toilet seats are the least of the military's crimes. And now the less developed countries are acquiring, by purchase from the big powers, modern military technology, at considerable opportunity cost in terms of meeting human and development needs. If we do not replace the war system with a system of international law and order under limited government, think of the waste that will be the result of a heavily militarized world.

The Club of Rome 1962 report on the limits to growth was easily shown to be defective in some respects, but, as others pointed out, it does not take a computer to know that there are limits on a finite planet. It is especially important to preserve the earth's topsoil, which we are not now doing. Population growth itself simply cannot proceed at any positive rate indefinitely. As it is, technology is not keeping ahead of such growth to keep Malthus in his grave, but it is aiding us in some quarters in overcropping, overgrazing, and overforesting the land, and in overfishing the seas, as the Worldwatch Institute publications document. The present world economy is not sustainable, and few economists have focused our attention in the textbooks on this as the real economic problem. One of the few who have tried to analyze how a sustainable economy might operate, and what changes in our thinking are needed accordingly, is Herman Daly.[25]

The Future Development
of Economics

38. What Picture of Social Problems?

Economics students tend to get a misleading view of social problems. Calling something a social problem entails a value judgment. Ordinarily the economist takes common judgments to define problems, although anyone is warranted in contending that some other things are unrecognized social problems. Economics principles textbooks typically start to make economists even out of students taking what is likely to be their only course in the subject. The books swamp them with so much technical analysis that there is not space even to identify the range of socioeconomic problems they may later recognize as people or try to deal with as citizens, problems that all have an important economic dimension.

Students who read some of the economics books that do pronounce on a whole range of such problems usually get answers to them in a few pages each, dealing with only one economic consideration apiece. It would give a much less misleading picture of social problems if each problem were outlined somewhat systematically in its true complexity. Then students would recognize that what the economist says about dealing with the problems is not a final word or conclusive or an all-sufficient guide, but only part of what needs to be considered. It is disturbing to find a very limited perspective being presented and taken as definitive. Economists are too often guilty of that.

A few specifics may be in order. Economics students, when given any information on what is often loosely termed the "farm problem," are likely to be given a brief application of supply-demand analysis to show that pegging an agricultural product price above equilibrium creates a surplus problem. Since agriculture is so basic to any economy, one might think that students deserve a brief picture also of its historical development, especially in their own country, and of the changing nature of problems faced by farmers, with emphasis on recent problems, plus a bit of critical analysis of the alternative ways they have been or could be dealt with. But most principles textbooks leave students thinking there is nothing in the area they ought to know about except that price supports are a mistake. They may not even learn why they won't do what some farmer advocates want to do. They probably do not learn why farm product price supports is a mistaken way to try to protect the family farm. They may or may not learn that price supports will not end farm poverty, since most of the payments go to large farmers. They do not learn from most principles of economics textbooks how extremely important soil conservation and soil depletion are. To deal only with the issue of price supports in agriculture leaves students in blatant ignorance of much that is of major importance to everyone in every economy. Every economics textbook should devote a whole large chapter to world agriculture and American agriculture.

Or take labor problems. The usual treatment is to talk about labor unions as interference in the wage determination market. Of course they should learn that the average real wages of labor depend primarily upon productivity, not union activity, unless somehow the labor share can thus be altered (despite lack of evidence that it can be). But no proper perspective is usually offered on the history and present state of the range of labor problems, management problems, and public problems in connection with labor-management relations. Unions have been quite important in dealing with arbitrary and unfair management practices, but one would not recognize that or its importance from usual textbook treatments of labor unions. They do not give a fair treatment of how this and other problems have been or could be dealt with. There is no question that entrepreneurship and business management are important, and economics deals with some of the decisions of business firms, including how much labor to hire. But after all, it is the labor employed in any firm that actually does most of the work and produces the products or services that the firm sells. Yet economics for the most part ignores all the problems of labor. It is as though people do not matter in production. Students of economics are given a simplistic and naive view of this whole important problem area by almost exclusive emphasis on labor unions as an interference in the labor market. Economics students can and do then go out and parrot what they were taught, not knowing how poor, limited, and misleading their insight is.

Consumer sovereignty is featured in the textbooks, but unless one takes a consumer economics course, which most economists look down upon and do not teach, a student would have no idea of the sovereign's problems that those disdained courses discuss. And one would have no idea of what is really involved in applying the economic principle to the range of normal household economic decisions. There is no hint of the general lessons that could be derived from *Consumer Reports* or from Nader's Raiders, despite the tendency of the Raiders to exaggerate. When students enter the world of work and of consumerism, if they have not done so already, they will discover, for example, that economics did not prepare them at all to know what to insure against or how to buy insurance in the actual insurance market. There are a few additional principles, besides marginalism, that they could have been given to prepare them for such practical decisions. Or as citizens they could have been given some insight into the issues of public policy in protection of buyers of large numbers of things from insurance or securities to pharmaceuticals and flammable children's sleepwear. All these matters and many more have very much to do with how sovereign the consumer is or can be. If production is conceived of as serving the consumers, serious discussion should center on the buyer's problems as among the shortcomings in the market that are typically ignored in principles texts. There could be and should be discussion of what to do about them. They could at least enter into some discussion in class of how to evaluate the advertising with which everybody is constantly deluged. The famous Samuelson textbook does not even list advertising in the index, and another says nothing about how to evaluate it.

Some problems do receive better attention, but not urban problems as such, despite an urbanized economy. To add location theory to standard textbooks would not suffice either. Urban problems certainly have an economic component, but to discuss them involves much more than economics. Perhaps that is why economics textbooks ignore them. But they are much more important for citizens to consider than nine-tenths of the diagrams described in detail in principles textbooks, which will be forgotten once the course is passed.

An economy's basic infrastructure is not even mentioned, except in passing as involved in economic development in the less developed countries. Such development, which should be shown to involve broad social development, not just more modern technology and capital, is clearly one of the big tasks now facing the human race, a task that may be rendered impossible if population growth does not halt at manageable levels.

The other major problems that the world must now face need to be highlighted when one takes any elementary social science course, which an economics course needs to be. Something should perhaps be stolen from Kenneth Boulding's little book, *The Meaning of the 20th Century*. It speaks of the world's need to escape the war trap, the poverty trap, and the energy trap, or the future may be bleak. It has an excellent brief analysis of the war problem. If we were even a semi-civilized society, we could eliminate war, as has been done over large areas now by appropriate demilitarization and the substitution of law and peaceful dispute settlement procedures. And though economies now depend heavily upon military expenditures, students can learn how reconversion can make everybody better off. Environmental problems are beginning to get more attention in economics textbooks, although even here with insufficient attention to both production and technologies regarding solar energy, pollution, and recycling. No economy is as yet even conceiving what may be necessary for it to achieve a sustainable basis. The population problem simply has to be faced over time, and as yet many people simply refuse to do so. Poverty is inexcusable in a society as wealthy as ours, a wealth to which less developed countries have every right to aspire. All these matters are more important for future citizens than such things as being able to diagram price discrimination profit maximization, something they are better prepared to do after a principles of economics course than to be intelligent citizens.

Attention to the really important issues that need to be faced will lead to consideration of how to conceive and measure progress in human well-being. It does not suffice simply to point out why GNP is an inadequate indicator, though that can start the inquiry. And economists' and popular worship of growth needs to be abandoned. Absolutely nothing so reduces human well-being, even economists' total utility, as much as violence in its many instances. Violence is not simply an economic problem, though the extreme economic individualism that economics fosters may increase violence. GNP does not include or exclude all that is needed to get a measure of real economic progress in contributing to human well-being. It should be replaced by a detailed profile enabling us to characterize progress or regress multidimensionally in each respect that matters. Some things will involve judgments rather than seemingly precise statistical measures. Every principles class should take some time to try to draw up such a profile to identify what is important in life and hence to an economy.

39. The Relation to Social Philosophy

Economists' views necessarily embody implicitly or explicitly a social philosophy. Textbooks should help students become aware of their own, and should help them reexamine them in the light of the social problems with which the future must deal. We all start with a natural individualism, reinforced by this culture and by the way economics is presented. Economics properly shows how the market economizes on consensus and harmonizes individual creativities to a remarkable extent. It does not induce students to recognize and wrestle seriously with the remainder of the problem. They can too easily think economics supports a business-is-business philosophy, which rules out all but profit-maximizing considerations, and explicitly excludes social and ethical considerations. Students can easily fail to see that any society needs to apply social criteria to all behavior and to all its institutions. They need a historical perspective on changes in the economy and changes in social philosophy about it. A bit of that is found in such a book as Frederick Lewis Allen's *The Big Change*. There should be, even at the textbook level, a bit of discussion of the need for some balance between individual freedoms and social norms, benefits and requirements. After all, some value consensus is needed to constitute a workable community and society. Current production is a result of all past and present productive effort—we build on all that went before. And a case can be made that what we do should be controlled in the interests of present and future producers, consumers, and citizens. There should be explicit consideration given to our relation to the framework within which a society's economy and political process operates. It should be made clear that there is no economic issue that does not involve an ethical issue, so economics alone cannot properly decide any issue. And students need to be helped to recognize that it is differences in their economic philosophies, as well as and often more important than their differences over economic theories, that divide economists on policy recommendations.

40. A Humanistic Economics Is Needed

The term "humanistic economics" is not new. There are fortunately a number of economists who have tried or are trying to develop, or point the way toward, such an economics. They propose to remedy some of the deficiencies in economics as they see them. They propose what in E.F. Schumacher's terms would be "economics as if people mattered." Everything that matters to humans is to be considered, not just what might maximize profits. Not all people involved are economists, and hopefully we can learn something from the others too.

Orthodox economics often assumes rationality, enough correct information, perfect competition as a norm, no barriers to entry, and complete factor mobility, and engages in comparative statistics analysis. John Maurice Clark once suggested that we should also explore what he terms "non-Euclidian" economics. It would take each of the major propositions of orthodox economics and indicate that there is a substantial degree of validity to be found in the opposite of each such proposition. He initiated such a task in one of his essays.[26] If economists generally were able even to contemplate such notions, it might inject just enough humility to cure them of the arrogant dogmatism that they are often guilty of in their pronouncements on what is an uneconomic policy.

We should recognize that orthodox economics is an "if . . . then" science, and as such tells us only the likely results of certain actions, given the cultural and institutional setting that is assumed and not described. This is not unimportant. It gives us causal statements that are of some help, though limited, in choosing means to our ends. But we also need to be aware of the fact that the world is more complicated than the economic models, and that other things will not in fact remain constant, so with economics we cannot predict outcomes. Indeed some of the assumptions made in developing the theories are wrong; that is, they are too unrealistic. In any case, a carefully thought-out social philosophy is needed to deal with real social issues, all of which involve ethical and other values. The social philosophy needs to embody economic principles carefully related to the various values relevant to any issue in any particular situation.

A recent important contribution toward humanizing economics comes from sociologist Amitai Etzioni's book *The Moral Dimension: Toward a New Economics*. He suggests substituting what he calls an "I and We" paradigm for what he calls the "neoclassical" paradigm. He thinks economics should go beyond treating all human behavior as pleasure or profit maximization and take into account the extent to which people are moral beings, with commitments to ethical principles. It is absurd, he says, to think that every unselfish act is part of pleasure maximization. He suggests that our norms and values other than economic should be given their rightful place in the analysis. While we can prescribe rationality, we need to go beyond rationality descriptively to take into account the large role played by human emotions. We need also to go beyond the individualism of economics and recognize the extent to which society enters into even our economic choices. And, as others have noted, economics has never adequately dealt with the role of power in economic relations.

As I have said above, our central efficiency concept needs serious redefinition in terms of human values, not just market values. That would change many economic judgments about what is efficient or inefficient, efficiency being the one value that economics recognizes. No rational case can be made for inefficiency. The question is what values should be served efficiently.

If some of these changes were made, the misleading simplicity of our economic models would disappear, and the reduction of social problems to overly simplistic economic dicta would cease.

Hopefully what the broadly humanistic economics may still need to say in terms of fundamental economics will not be underrated or lost in the complications and various values that are now too often ignored in economic pronouncements.

Perhaps economics needs to add to its concepts of physical and human capital the concept of social capital. That consists of those operative and effective social norms that facilitate social trust and cooperation for the common good. There was a day when everyone in a neighborhood knew each other, and the "community raised the children." Such a community was not violent, nor did it generally disregard the well-being of its members for mere economic gain for someone. The mobility of our economy makes that difficult, but the almost exclusively individualistic ideology of economics is also contributing to the disappearance of our social capital, not to its maintenance. For a long time the Christian ethic remained influential enough to undergird the capitalistic economies, contributing to their workability and progress, but its hold is continuously weakening in many quarters. Communist ideology required an even more socially oriented ethic to work well, but in practice communists relied upon totalitarian force instead. So now when its economic system is in transition, it lacks the social capital that would alone make the transition workable, and enters the chaos of too many for themselves and too few for the common good. What is called corruption in any system is merely economic individualism run rampant, without the restraining force of social norms of behavior. Building community, building social capital is more difficult than building physical or human capital, but in the end it is even more basic to the economic and social process. Developing good citizenship and concern for the common good, and not so much for one's own greed or power hunger, is the biggest need in our day in all countries. Economics needs to be reformed to make such things as the great importance of social capital clear to all.

Social capital gets embedded in people's consciences as they grow up. Consciences define injustice as most people in society see it at any given time. Production for a market is carried on by businesses of all sizes, from the individual operator to the huge holding company in which responsibilities are somewhat hard to pin down. When social capital is weakened, business does not always operate in the general social interest. That social interest is not as hard to define as some political scientists seem to think it is even in an obviously pluralistic society. When the social interest is not well served, only government can operate as a corrective. And even a democracy finds it difficult for government to serve the social interest when elections depend heavily upon financing by the businesses that need to be regulated.

The more and the stronger "social capital" is, the less need there is of government regulation to induce business to operate in the social interest. Business conscience and the social conscience of others does much to take care of the stakeholder problem. Government regulation is needed only for the marginal cases where social conscience is deficient.

Excessive individualism and profit maximization without regard to the social consequences represent the lack or breakdown of social capital. Although many prominent economists went into the field with a concern for the poor, economists have largely become the high priests of such pure, undiluted, and excessive individualism. They need to recognize that business is justifiable only when it operates in the general social interest as represented by all business stakeholders. Economists should become the high priests of humanistic economics, of human and social well-being, of social capital rather than merely of those we now readily identify as big capital owners. Economics as it is now taught is almost an antisocial discipline. Economists need to change their tune. Instead of being apologists for whatever goes toward profit maximization in the markets that business wants unregulated, we should identify the public interest, call for consciences to serve it, and, where needed, call for government to regulate the economy in the public interest.

Economics supposes itself to be a science of the rational relation of means to given ends. But it takes the ends of business to be simply profit maximization, short run or long run, without regard to stakeholders. And for others, the end is defined by a preference ordering, but only among the goods and services that business provides in a market. Theoretically there is also a choice between leisure and work, but for most of us that is practically constrained by the jobs business provides.

An earlier essay dealt with real human ends and how they can be objectively defined. They are dominated by the quality of our relations with other human beings. Our individual well-being is not isolated. Unless we have escaped a social conscience, our preference ordering knows that and is far broader than the market. It is time for economists to recognize that and teach economics to account for it. A humanistic economics would be concerned with the rational and efficient pursuit of the ends that have been learned to really promote individual and social well-being. The quality of human relations on the job would have to receive a lot of attention as an end, not just a means to profitability.

Of course natural human individualism and egoism need outlets, but outlets that involve harmonizing our creativities with the creativities of others, with our community and society in general, with the entire environment, and with the whole complex world of which we are a part. It is that harmonization of all human creativities for which economists should be among the high priests, not for any more limited perspective that encourages egoism without regard to its sometimes partly unfortunate consequences.

The organized specialization in the business economies that have developed has vastly increased human economic interdependencies. That coupled with a tremendous burst of science-based inventiveness has greatly increased human productivity in many goods and services. The interdependencies also entail increased economic insecurities to add to the various other insecurities of life.

At the same time, interdependence opens up opportunities to deal with the insecurities in ways otherwise not possible. Both privately sold insurance and social insurance give protection that cannot possibly be achieved by private saving. There is no reason why business should be saddled with pensions for people no longer working or for health insurance other than worker's compensation insurance (for job-related diseases and accidents). Business should try to get these two burdens shifted to social insurance. That is the only way they can be handled adequately. No one can know in advance their financial need in either respect, so private savings simply cannot suffice. Anyone who understands insurance principles at all—principles that economics fails to incorporate as it should—knows that much.

So even elementary economics textbooks could do much better than they do for students. While its diagrams are very helpful, it could eliminate many of the more complicated ones, which are of interest only to economists, in order to spend more time on more important matters such as have been discussed here. A humanistic economics as suggested here is what is really needed.

The proper role of an elementary principles of economics course is not to begin the training of professional economists, but to help students acquire some appreciation of how economic principles should have an important but very limited role in important personal and social decisions.

Notes

1. John M. Clark, *Preface to Social Economics: Essays on Economic Theory and Social Problems.*

2. See the Economics entry written by Edwin R.A. Seligman in his *Encyclopedia of the Social Sciences.*

3. Herbert Simon, *Reason in Human Affairs.*

4. Amitai Etzioni, *The Moral Dimension: Toward a New Economics.*

5. For a simple review of Maslow's pyramid, see Mark A. Lutz and Kenneth Lux, *The Challenge of Humanistic Economics.*

6. E.F. Schumacher, *Small Is Beautiful: Economics as if People Mattered.*

7. John Hobson, *Work and Wealth: A Human Valuation.*

8. Adam Smith, *The Theory of Moral Sentiments,* and *An Inquiry into the Nature and Causes of the Wealth of Nations.*

9. Lester Thurow, *Dangerous Currents: The State of Economics.*

10. Ibid.

11. Bruno Frey, *Economics as a Science of Human Behavior.*

12. Herbert Simon, *Reason in Human Affairs.*

13. John Maynard Keynes, *The General Theory of Employment, Interest and Money,* p. 383.

14. Eduardo Gianetti da Fonseca, *Beliefs in Action: Economic Philosophy and Social Change.*

15. Thomas Balogh, *The Irrelevance of Conventional Economics.*

16. Barbara Wootton, *Lament for Economics.*

17. Ibid.

18. Lester Thurow, *Dangerous Currents: The State of Economics.*

19. Barlett and Steele, *America: What Went Wrong?*

20. See Thurman Arnold, *The Folklore of Capitalism.*

21. Lester Thurow, *Dangerous Currents: The State of Economics.*

22. John E. Schwarz, *America's Hidden Success: A Reassessment of Public Policy from Kennedy to Reagan.*

23. Robert Kuttner, *The End of Laissez-Faire: National Purpose and the Global Economy After the Cold War.*

24. E.F. Schumacher, *Small Is Beautiful: Economics as if People Mattered.*

25. Herman Daly, *Steady-State Economics.*

26. John M. Clark, *Preface to Social Economics: Essays on Economic Theory and Social Problems.*

Bibliography

Allen, Frederick L. *The Big Change: America Transforms Itself, 1900–1950.* New York: Harper and Row, 1988.

Arnold, Thurman. *The Folklore of Capitalism.* New Haven: Yale University Press, 1937.

Balinky, Alexander. *Marx's Economics: Overview and Development.* Lexington, MA: D.C. Heath, 1970.

Balogh, Thomas. *The Irrelevance of Conventional Economics.* New York: Liveright, 1982.

Barlett, Donald L., and James B. Steele. *America: What Went Wrong?* Kansas City: Andrews and McMeel, 1992.

Berle, A.A., and Gardiner C. Means. *The Modern Corporation and Private Property,* rev. ed. New York: Harcourt, Brace and World, 1968.

Boulding, Kenneth E. *The Meaning of the 20th Century: The Great Transition.* Lanham, MD: University Press of America, 1988.

Business Week.

Carroll, Archie B. *Business and Society: Ethics and Stakeholder Management,* 3d ed. Cincinnati: South-Western College Publishers, 1996.

Clark, John M. *Preface to Social Economics: Essays on Economic Theory and Social Problems.* New York: Farrar and Rinehart, 1936.

Consumer Reports.

da Fonseca, Eduardo Giannetti. *Beliefs in Action: Economic Philosophy and Social Change.* New York: Cambridge University Press, 1991.

Daly, Herman E. *Steady-State Economics, Second Edition, with New Essays.* Washington, DC: Island Press, 1991.

Etzioni, Amitai. *The Moral Dimension: Toward a New Economics.* New York: Free Press; London: Collier Macmillan, 1988.

Frey, Bruno. *Economics as a Science of Human Behavior.* Boston: Kluwer Academic, 1992.

Galbraith, John Kenneth. *The Affluent Society.* Boston: Houghton Mifflin, 1958.

George, Henry. *Progress and Poverty.* New York: Harcourt, Brace, 1924.

Goodpaster, Kenneth E., John B. Matthews, and Laura L. Nash. *Policies and Persons: A Casebook in Business Ethics,* 2d ed. New York: McGraw-Hill, 1991.

Hobson, J.A. *Work and Wealth: A Human Valuation.* New York: Macmillan, 1921.

Keynes, John Maynard. *The General Theory of Employment, Interest and Money.* New York: Harcourt, Brace, 1936.

Kuttner, Robert. *The Economic Illusion: False Choices between Prosperity and Social Justice.* Philadelphia: University of Pennsylvania Press, 1987.

———. *The End of Laissez-Faire: National Purpose and the Global Economy after the Cold War.* New York: Knopf, 1991.

———. *Everything for Sale: The Virtues and Limits of Markets.* New York: Knopf, 1997.

Lutz, Mark A., and Kenneth Lux. *The Challenge of Humanistic Economics.* Menlo Park, CA: Benjamin/Cummings, 1979.

Malthus, Thomas R. *An Essay on the Principle of Population.* Oxford: Oxford University Press, 1993.

Okun, Arthur M. *Equality and Efficiency: The Big Tradeoff.* Washington, DC: The Brookings Institution, 1975.

Rawls, John. *A Theory of Justice.* Cambridge: Harvard University Press, 1971.

Schumacher, E.F. *Small Is Beautiful: Economics as if People Mattered.* New York: Harper Colophon Books, 1975.

Schumpeter, Joseph A. *Business Cycles: A Theoretical, Historical and Statistical Analysis of the Capitalist Process.* Philadelphia: Porcupine Press, 1982.

Schwarz, John E. *America's Hidden Success: A Reassessment of Public Policy from Kennedy to Reagan,* rev. ed. New York: Norton, 1988.

Seligman, Edwin R.A., ed. *Encyclopedia of the Social Sciences.* New York: Macmillan, 1930.

Simon, Herbert A. *Reason in Human Affairs.* Stanford: Stanford University Press, 1983.

Smith, Adam. *An Inquiry into the Nature and Causes of the Wealth of Nations.* Oxford: Oxford University Press, 1993.

———. *The Theory of Moral Sentiments.* New York: Oxford University Press, 1976.

Thurow, Lester C. *Dangerous Currents: The State of Economics.* New York: Vintage Books, 1984.

Ward, Barbara. *Rich Nations and Poor Nations.* New York: Norton, 1962.

Wootton, Barbara. *Lament for Economics.* New York: Farrar and Rinehart, 1938.

Index

About the Author

Harlan M. Smith is Economics Professor Emeritus at the University of Minnesota. He has taught micro and macro theory, monetary, international, and development economics.